PALM
/////////SIZED PLAN

First published in 2011 by Buckingham Book Publishing Ltd
Network House, 28 Ballmoor, Celtic Court,
Buckingham MK18 1RQ, UK
www.chefmagazine.co.uk
© Buckingham Book Publishing Ltd

ISBN No: 978-0-9567667-0-0

Publisher: Peter Marshall
Managing Editor: Shirley Marshall
Editor: Katy Morris
Assistant Editor: Sue Christelow
Design Director: Philip Donnelly
Graphic Designer: Duncan Boddy
Photographer: Myburgh du Plessis
Jonny Wilkinson photography courtesy of Getty Images®

THANKS

I'd like to thank a few people who have helped make this book happen, without them this book would have been impossible.

My beautiful wife **Josie** and my wonderful children **Alfie** and **Sophia** who provide the happiness, back-bone and rocks to support my jetty going out into the ocean, making life a truly wonderful adventure. To **Freddy Brown** for his continued friendship, hard work and inspiration, you need people like him to keep you sharp. To **Ray Klerck** who made the science understandable through his magic powders. I'd also like to thank **Gavin Allinson** for his continued support, friendship and dedication, helping me to steer the ship forwards.

My sister **Hannah** for all her help with this project. The guys at **Buckingham Book Publishing** who are a force of nature and without whom I wouldn't have been able to get all this done, **Myburgh**, **Duncan**, **Katy**, **Glenn** and **Peter**. And last but not least my mum **Vivien** who gave me inspiration in the kitchen as I'd watch her preparing our supper, chatting so many evenings, and my father **Haakon** for his eastern influences and more inspiration in the kitchen.

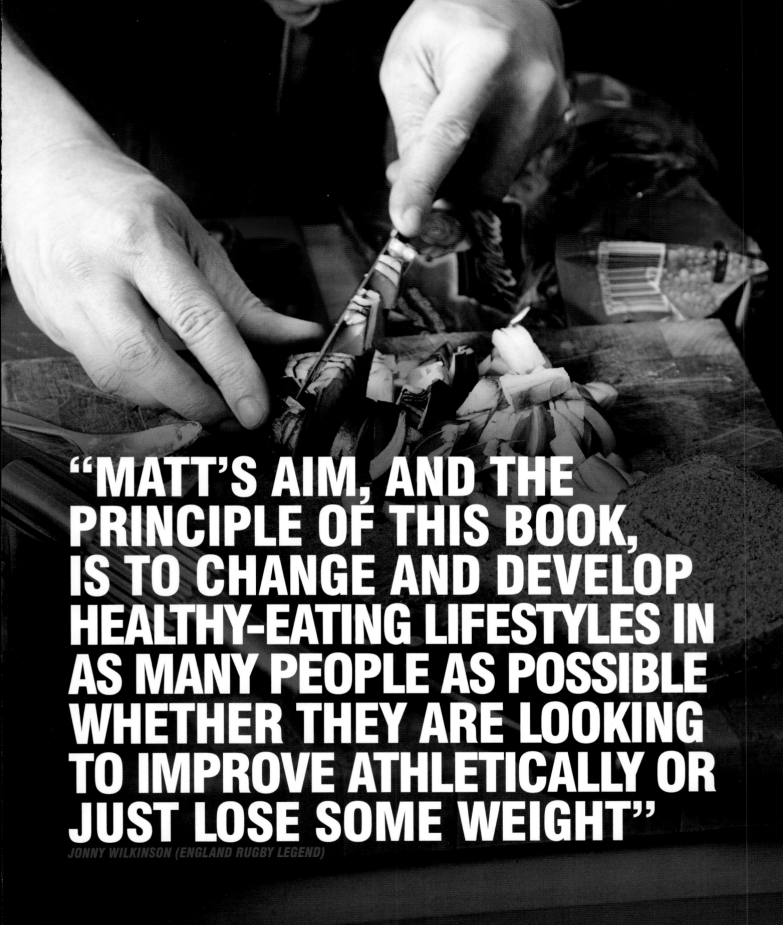

"MATT'S AIM, AND THE PRINCIPLE OF THIS BOOK, IS TO CHANGE AND DEVELOP HEALTHY-EATING LIFESTYLES IN AS MANY PEOPLE AS POSSIBLE WHETHER THEY ARE LOOKING TO IMPROVE ATHLETICALLY OR JUST LOSE SOME WEIGHT"

JONNY WILKINSON (ENGLAND RUGBY LEGEND)

<FOREWORD>

FOREWORD* – BY JONNY WILKINSON

"IT GIVES ME GREAT PLEASURE TO WRITE THE FOREWORD FOR THIS COOKBOOK DUE TO THE ENORMOUSLY POSITIVE MESSAGE IT CONTAINS WITHIN.

Food and nutrition, and all the bits that go with it, has always been, and still is, a major influence in my life and goals. In fact, it is so closely interwoven within all that I do – and want to achieve – that I often find it impossible to distinguish between what is preparing to perform to your best and what is actually being at your best.

In my eyes, how you look after your body and yourself goes a long way towards defining who you are and what you are really about. It speaks volumes about how you see life and what sort of a difference you feel you can make in it. I didn't really feel or act this way before I met Matt and he has helped me see things differently. I had definitely tried to do the right things up until that point some 10 or more years ago but I was missing the mark and consequently missing out.

Matt through his professionalism, his knowledge, his desire to research deeper and ultimately, his friendship, has given me an extra level in my career and more importantly in my daily life. With inappropriate and often insufficient nutritional routines and support I used to waste so much of the hard work I put into my training and my preparation because I didn't know what to eat or when to eat around my tough workouts – now with his help, I maximise the effects.

Working towards the goal of finding my true potential, together Matt and I have explored some interesting avenues. Whether it be the cookies and cream flavour protein shakes that I love, the Chinese-style liquorice herbs that lift my moods or the shots of beetroot which help me recover as I get older in this game it's all been a revelation. More importantly it has been his fairly simple and very sound advice that I have benefitted from the most.

Supplying your body with what it needs to flourish is often a bit of a personal thing. There are some solid principles which, once in place, make it quite difficult to go wrong – but we are all different and we need to find what works best for

"IN MY EYES, HOW YOU LOOK AFTER YOUR BODY AND YOURSELF GOES A LONG WAY TOWARDS DEFINING WHO YOU ARE AND WHAT YOU ARE REALLY ABOUT"
JONNY WILKINSON (ENGLAND RUGBY LEGEND)

ourselves. By using the helpful advice he gives and through trialling and testing, you too can find the formula for supporting and living a brilliant and fulfilling life.

Matt's aim, and the principal of this book, is to change and develop healthy-eating lifestyles in as many people as possible whether they are looking to improve athletically or just lose some weight. Most importantly it is aimed at bringing out the very best of you so that you can enjoy your life to the fullest.

I mentioned earlier that what you eat and how and when you eat it, can dictate your life, so use the information in this book to make your life a great one, filled with energy. Give yourself the chance to do and see amazing things, make your life as fulfilled as possible by looking after your body and by continuing to fuel and refuel your dreams."

Jonny Wilkinson (England Rugby Legend)

<CONTENTS>

"BE GOOD IN THE WEEK, GO EASY ON THE WEEKENDS AND USE THE PALM OF YOUR HAND AS A GUIDE TO PORTION SIZES"

MATT LOVELL (TOP SPORTS NUTRITIONIST)

CONTENTS

< INTRODUCTION >

"WHEN I WROTE THIS BOOK I WAS THINKING OF YOU – ALL THE PEOPLE OUT THERE WITH POTENTIAL PROBLEMS AND ISSUES COOKING, EATING AND SOURCING HEALTHY FOODS"

MATT LOVELL (TOP SPORTS NUTRITIONIST)

INTRODUCTION*

I'M HAPPY TO BE GIVING YOU THIS INFORMATION WHICH I HOPE HELPS YOU BECOME HEALTHIER, LEANER AND FREE FROM ILLNESS.

WHEN I WROTE THIS BOOK I WAS THINKING OF YOU – ALL THE PEOPLE OUT THERE WITH POTENTIAL PROBLEMS AND ISSUES COOKING, EATING AND SOURCING HEALTHY FOODS, ENJOYING THEM AND DOING ALL THIS WITH BUSY WORK, FAMILY AND TRAINING SCHEDULES. THE RECIPES ARE ALL DOABLE – QUICK TO PREPARE AND THE FORMAT CONSIDERS YOUR WEEK, YOUR PLANS AND EVEN SOME OF THE MORE SOCIAL OR COMFORT-BASED DISHES YOU MAY WANT TO COOK.

THE RECIPES ARE WRITTEN IN REAL TIME AND BASED ON INGREDIENTS YOU CAN FIND EASILY OR ORDER ONLINE. THE PINK AND GREEN RECIPES GIVE A STRAIGHTFORWARD VIEW OF RECIPES WITH EITHER A HIGHER CARB PROPORTION OR HIGHER PROTEIN CONTENT. THE NUTRITIONAL VALUES CAN BE FOUND IN THE CORNER OF EACH PAGE AND ARE BASED ON AN AVERAGE PERSON'S PROTEIN, FAT AND CARBOHYDRATE CONTENT. AS YOU READ FURTHER INTO THE BOOK YOU WILL EVENTUALLY BE ABLE TO WORK OUT YOUR OWN PERSONAL RECOMMENDED DAILY AMOUNTS USING THE PALM OF YOUR HAND AND THEN TAILOR RECIPES TO FIT.

IN THE RECIPE SECTION I'VE TRIED TO FOCUS ON OLD CLASSICS ALONG WITH SOME OF THE NATION'S (AND MY OWN) FAVOURITE DISHES, ALL WITH ORGANICALLY SOURCED, LOCALLY PRODUCED AND SEASONAL INGREDIENTS. I STRONGLY BELIEVE THAT THE NUTRITIONAL ELEMENTS ARE ONLY AS GOOD AS THE QUALITY OF INGREDIENTS USED – THEREFORE I RECOMMEND ORGANIC OR FREE-RANGE OMEGA-3 EGGS WHERE POSSIBLE AND HOME-MADE ALTERNATIVES FOR CONDIMENTS SUCH AS TOMATO KETCHUP OR AT LEAST AN ORGANIC, CONTROLLED SUGAR ALTERNATIVE.

THE BASIS BEHIND THIS BOOK MEANS THAT YOU CAN GIVE UP THE FAD DIETS AND REALLY GO BACK TO BASICS, BE GOOD IN THE WEEK, GO EASY ON THE WEEKENDS AND USE THE PALM OF YOUR HAND AS A GUIDE TO PORTION SIZES – THROW IN SOME REGULAR EXERCISE AND IT'S A LIFE PLAN.

MATT LOVELL

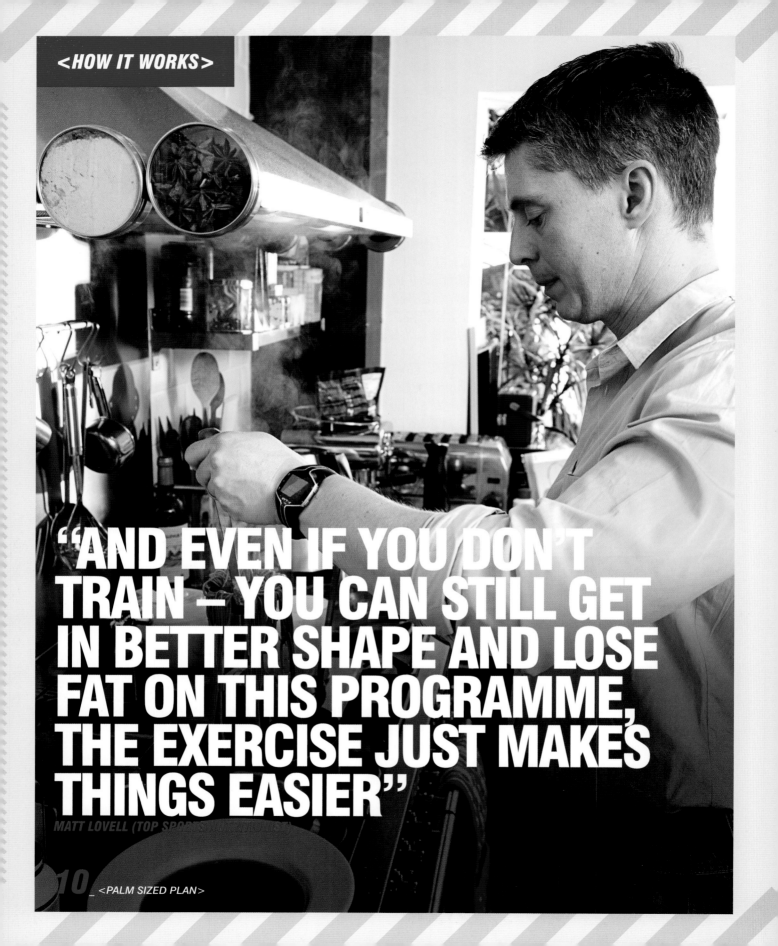

"AND EVEN IF YOU DON'T TRAIN – YOU CAN STILL GET IN BETTER SHAPE AND LOSE FAT ON THIS PROGRAMME, THE EXERCISE JUST MAKES THINGS EASIER"

MATT LOVELL (TOP SPORTS NUTRITIONIST)

HOW IT WORKS*

IF LOSING WEIGHT IS A GAME, THE INFORMATION YOU'RE ABOUT TO READ IS YOUR PLAYBOOK FOR WINNING. YOU MAY ALREADY KNOW THE RULES, BUT THESE ARE THE SOLID PRINCIPLES THAT YOU CAN APPLY TO EVERY RECIPE AND OVEREATING SITUATION YOU'RE LIKELY TO BE FACED WITH. THEY'LL PUT YOU FIRMLY IN CHARGE OF YOUR KNIFE AND FORK AND TEACH YOU HOW TO ADAPT TO THE NEEDS AND DEMANDS OF YOUR EXERCISE REGIME AND LIFE. AND EVEN IF YOU DON'T TRAIN – YOU CAN STILL GET IN BETTER SHAPE AND LOSE FAT ON THIS PROGRAMME, THE EXERCISE JUST MAKES THINGS EASIER AND IDEALLY IS PART OF BECOMING HEALTHIER.

THE IDEA BEHIND THIS COOKBOOK IS CENTRED AROUND THREE MAIN PRINCIPLES:

> **COLOUR CODING FOODS** – DEPENDING ON CALORIE/ CARBOHYDRATE CONTENT.

> **PORTION CONTROL** – EATING THE RIGHT AMOUNT OF FOODS FOR YOUR DESIRED WEIGHT.

> **THE WEEKLY SCHEDULE** – HOW THE ABOVE WORK IN YOUR DAILY ROUTINE.

COLOUR CODING

PINK DISHES

Portion control is the key to managing healthy body fat percentages. To help you with this, the recipes in this book are colour coded according to their nutrient and energy density. If a dish contains starchy carbs or is a high energy dish, the code will be **PINK**. This means that eating too much of these foods without enough exercise to balance them out may make dropping fat difficult.

Even though **PINK** meals are still healthy, they have the potential to slow your fat loss if your energy balance is not in favour of body fat reduction. These are meals that although still balanced would be more inclined to maintain a healthy weight and your current fat percentage, again if not eaten to excess.

GREEN DISHES

The lower energy density dishes are coded **GREEN** which is designed to assist with the dropping of body fat as well as keeping you feeling full for a while afterwards. An example of this might be the Miso soup – by adding noodles into the soup it increases the energy density of this meal and adds significantly more calories, thus making it a **PINK** dish.

CHANGING THE COLOUR OF A DISH

You can change the colour code of a dish if you simply eat too much of it – the larger the portions the larger the insulin response. Equally, eating a smaller portion of a **PINK** dish can give you a **GREEN** code. Generally, if your food is no larger than two hands cupped and is made up of protein, carbs and good fat then it'll stay **GREEN** – if it's just fat and sugar it should be eaten only as a treat.

To know which meals to stick to, see below:

> A. THE NATURALLY LEAN PERSON

Be more generous with carbohydrate intake. This means eating more of the **PINK** dishes in the recipe section. Exercising once per day or every 24 hours makes a high carbohydrate intake less important – if this is the case eating high quality proteins and regular meals will be enough to help you recover. You can eat according to the palms for portions guidelines for your present body weight, explained further in this chapter.

> B. THE PERSON LOOKING TO GET LEANER

If fat loss is your main concern keep to the **GREEN** dishes in the recipe section, even after you exercise. Choose the palms for portions if your desired body weight is not the weight that you are currently.

> C. THE ATHLETE

If you train more than once per day you'll need liquid recovery drinks including plentiful protein drinks – the smoothie recipes in this book fit this bill perfectly. You'll need to eat **PINK** dishes, protein smoothies and work out your total daily energy requirements and then match the recipes to your daily needs.

PORTION CONTROL

You can see on the colour coding system that to stay trim simply eat **GREEN** and keep to two hands cupped together for a whole meal or use your palms for portions in the below chart for your desired lean weight.

The table below shows how many grams of fat, carbohydrates and protein you need in your day in order to move towards your desired weight. You can find out your size in grams by multiplying your desired body weight (BW) by 2 or 1 (as specified below) and then dividing this amount by four daily meals.

> FOR EXAMPLE:

For a person wanting to weigh 50kg they need a protein amount of 25g per meal. In order to get 28.5g of protein they need to eat around 1 palm or 100g of chicken.

DESIRED WEIGHT (BW)	PROTEIN PALMS = BW x 2 divided by 4 daily meals	CARB PALMS = BW X 1 DIVIDED BY 4 DAILY MEALS	FAT THUMB = BW X 1 DIVIDED BY 4 DAILY MEALS
50KG	**25g per meal** **1 palm** 100g / 28.5g (based on chicken breast fillet)	**12.5g per meal** **3 palms** 300g / 14g (based on broccoli)	**12.5g per meal** **1 thumb for liquids** 1 tablespoon / 15g (based on olive oil) **2 thumbs for hard fats** 2 tablespoons / 10g (based on almonds)
60KG	**30g per meal** **1 palms** 200g / 34.24g (based on ham, not canned)	**15g per meal** **3 palms** 300g / 15g (based on cauliflower)	**15g per meal** **1 thumb for liquids** 1 tablespoon / 15g (based on coconut oil) **1 palm** 100g / 14.66g (based on avocado flesh)
70KG	**35g per meal** **1 palm** 100g / 31.06g (based on lean beef steak)	**17.5g per meal** **4 palms** 400g / 15.52g (based on asparagus)	**17.5g per meal** **2 thumbs for liquids** 2 tablespoons / 22g (based on butter) **¼ palm** 25g / 16.5g (based on Brazil nuts)
80KG	**40g per meal** **1½ palms** 150g / 39g (based on tuna, canned in water, drained solids)	**20g per meal** **1½ palms** 150g / 21.75g (based on peas)	**20g per meal** **3 thumbs for liquids** 3 tablespoons / 22.02g (based on pesto sauce)
90KG	**45g per meal** **2¼ palms** 225g / 45.70g (based on uncooked prawns)	**22.5g per meal** **6 palms** 600g / 21.6g (based on raw spinach)	**22.5g per meal** **²/₃ palm** 67g / 22g (based on cheddar cheese)
100KG	**50g per meal** **3 palms** 300g / 54g (based on raw Pacific cod)	**25g per meal** **1 palm** 100g / 23g (based on long-grain brown rice, cooked)	**25g per meal** **2 thumbs for liquids** 2 tablespoons / 28g (based on walnut oil) **½ palm** 50g / 32.5g (based on walnuts)
110KG	**55g per meal** **3 palms** 300g / 54.87g (based on fresh crab)	**27.5g per meal** **12 palms** 1200g / 28g (based on mixed salad leaves)	**27.5g per meal** **2 thumbs for liquids** 2 tablespoons / 28g (based on sesame oil) **½ palm** 50g / 24.5g (based on dried pumpkin seeds)

You can also use this food exchange chart to modify recipes from the book or to create your own meals.

The below is just a guide and you can amend it according to the desired weight amounts in the portion table opposite.

PROTEIN	VEGETABLE	FAT
1 palm per meal	4 palms per meal	1 thumb liquid 2 thumbs for solids per meal
Chicken	Alfalfa sprouts*	Almonds
Turkey	Artichoke	Almond butter
Lamb	Asparagus	Avocado
Halibut	Beetroot	Cashews
Cod	Peppers	Flaxseeds
Tuna	Bok choy	Olive oil
Salmon	Broccoli	Pecans
Mackerel	Brussels sprouts	Pumpkin seeds
Wild game	Cabbage	Sesame seeds
Omega eggs	Cauliflower	Sunflower seeds
Protein powder	Celery*	Walnuts
	Courgette	
	Cucumber*	
	Radish*	
	Kale	
	Leeks	
	Lettuce*	
	Mushroom*	
	Okra	
	Onions	
	Spinach	
	Water chestnut	

* These are foods that are essentially 'free' in that you can eat as much of these as you wish.

WHAT TO DO?

If it's not on the list above, that doesn't mean you shouldn't eat it. There may be other foods closely related the food groups that you can eat. So exotic meats such as ostrich, buffalo and antelope can of course be substituted for the ole humdrum cow. Here's the good part: you can eat unlimited amounts of herbs and spices of all descriptions. So your journey doesn't have to be a flavour-free affair.

One caveat – if you are one of those people who are really small with really BIG hands you need to go for the grams instead, similarly if you are really big but nature handed you a small pair of mittens – use the grams instead to make up your portions.

Once you've weighed stuff out a couple of times it's really easy and you'll be able to do it by eye after that, arming yourself with skill-power over willpower.

GETTING USED TO PORTION SIZES

The most important thing is to stick to eating at set times with set portion sizes. For your desired body weight see the portions sizes above and enforce them or get a friend or significant other to do portion control for you.

Scoops are a really easy way to get used to measuring portions as you only have to weigh them out once and then you can use specific scoops for portions.

For instance, a 40g portion of porridge oats (150 Kcal) can be easily measured by filling a ½ pint beer-glass to the 'bulge' about two-thirds of the way up. Once you've counted out a few portions it'll seem like second nature. Plus you can also eat free-eating foods such as lettuce, bean sprouts, celery and mushrooms in as much volume as you wish.

THE RECIPES IN THIS COOKBOOK ARE JUST A GUIDE BASED ON THE MEASURES AN AVERAGE PERSON SHOULD EAT. EVENTUALLY AS YOU START TO COOK THEM MORE AND MORE YOU CAN AMEND THE AMOUNTS BASED ON THE PALM CONTROLLED PORTIONS MENTIONED ABOVE.

THE WEEKLY SCHEDULE

The plan is simple – you eat healthily for five days – then spend the weekends doing what you want to with some simple limitations – none of which will dent your fun-o-meter. Most people give up on diets because they're too restrictive, are loaded with too much bland food or because they never let you cut loose and enjoy life. This plan includes delicious foods and changes the way you eat – rather than putting you on a diet. It lets you reload and relax on the weekends and during the week is also pretty good fun to be honest.

FOLLOW THESE GUIDELINES TO GET STARTED.

STEP 1: Two days of planning and preparation. Do this over the weekend and get rid of poor foods, go shopping, give up alcohol and sweets and start training.

STEP 2: Begin the 3-day detox.

STEP 3: Adopt a high protein and vegetable phase for 2 days then eat as normal on the weekend.

STEP 4: Your 5-day plan begins on Monday and runs to Friday. This is where you'll stick to purely GREEN dishes and will avoid exercise on Wednesdays. Only eat PINK dishes after training. It's as simple as that.

STEP 5: The weekend. Eat what you like or for faster fat loss eat GREEN dishes all week.

3-DAY DETOX

To start off your plan and get you off to a flying motivational beginning you're going to reset your cells to become fat-burning furnaces. The best part: you're going to do this in 72 hours. Studies have shown that success in the first two weeks of changing the way you eat dramatically influences your sticking ability and adherence later on during your plan. So keep to it, no matter how hard it is. Here's what you do:

MONDAY	TUESDAY	WEDNESDAY
Drink hot water with half a lemon and 1 teaspoon of honey. You can make this with green tea if you wish	Drink hot water with half a lemon and 1 teaspoon of honey. You can make this with green tea if you wish	Drink hot water with half a lemon and 1 teaspoon of honey. You can make this with green tea if you wish
Juice 1 whole lemon, 1 kiwi, a handful of ginger and 1 apple – dilute with water and sip gradually	Juice 1 whole lemon, 1 kiwi, a handful of ginger and 1 apple – dilute with water and sip gradually	Juice 1 whole lemon, 1 kiwi, a handful of ginger and 1 apple – dilute with water and sip gradually
Take a handful of ginger, 1 lemon, 1 kiwi and 1 carrot together with 1 dessertspoon of psyllium husk and dilute with 50% water and 1 serving of greens	Take a handful of ginger, 1 lemon, 1 kiwi and 1 carrot together with 1 dessertspoon of psyllium husk and dilute with 50% water and 1 serving of greens	Take a handful of ginger, 1 lemon, 1 kiwi and 1 carrot together with 1 dessertspoon of psyllium husk and dilute with 50% water and 1 serving of greens
Eat a meal of salad – see allowed salad vegetables plus a source of allowed proteins	Eat a meal of salad – see allowed salad vegetables plus a source of allowed proteins	Eat a meal of salad – see allowed salad vegetables plus a source of allowed proteins
Eat a meal of cooked vegetables or soups with a source of cooked proteins	Eat a meal of cooked vegetables or soups with a source of cooked proteins	Eat a meal of cooked vegetables or soups with a source of cooked proteins

N.B. Psyllium husks are available from your local health food shop and add fibre to your diet without calories.

Using the portion size guide you can tailor these meals to your desired weight. Exercise wise you can do what you normally do but expect some decrease in endurance if that's your form of training.

If you enjoy the 3-day-detox then you can stick with it for as long as you want – the ideal time to stick to the plan is 4-6 weeks. After this you can switch to a maintenance phase where you can relax your strictness on the weekends a bit more.

AFTER THE DETOX

For Thursday and Friday of your detox follow the examples below:

THURSDAY	FRIDAY
3 Eggs and spinach omelette Green tea	Tuna and chilli frittata Black coffee
15 Almonds and ½ pot of 0% yoghurt	½ Pot of cottage cheese
Prawn salad	Tom yum soup (no noodles)
Protein shake	Protein bar
Steak and broccoli	Baked sea bass

All of the meals from the above are GREEN and you can exchange them for other GREEN coded meals in the book if you want to keep the detox going for longer.

THE FOLLOWING WEEKS

Over the following weeks the plan is easy – if you are planning to lose weight your four daily meals need to be chosen from the GREEN coded meals. Directly after you exercise you can choose any of the PINK coloured meals and then at the weekends you can choose from a mixture of the two and basically eat what you like – just don't pull a deck-chair to the fridge.

If you follow the palms for portions guidelines and don't stuff your face you'll gradually drop fat weight with little difficulty with or without exercise. You'll be able to enjoy your weekends and amaze your friends how lean and muscled you can be while enjoying the foods you love.

If you are hoping to improve your performance follow the portion plan for your desired weight and stick to the PINK meals.

Follow the weekly tips below to help you stick to your plan.

SATURDAY

Do what you like – eat what you like but keep to foods you enjoy rather than going out of your way to eat rubbish.

Try to have just one total blow out on each day.

Take two shakes containing protein according to your body weight – 0.4g protein per kg of body weight.

You don't have to train on the weekends but it is recommended. It's important to do something Sunday night if you've had a weekend of over-indulgence.

SUNDAY

Do what you like – eat what you like but aim to do as Saturday but maybe do some light activity such as walking.

Have a hearty Sunday lunch and do your Sunday cooking routine. Train at night ideally to prepare your body for fat burning Monday morning.

Eat some carbs after this session 0.3g / kg in addition to normal carb allowance.

MONDAY

Eat protein and fibrous vegetables only – all day.

Drink plenty of water.

Exercise again at night and after the pm session have a protein and salad dish (such as the prawn cocktail).

TUESDAY

Eat protein and fibrous vegetables only – all day.

Drink plenty of water.

Exercise again at night and have a protein and salad dish.

WEDNESDAY

No training today unless you really fancy it.

Eat some additional carbs today – but no more than 1g / kg in addition to your weekday allowance.

Use soups / root vegetable based – or some slow release fruits but aim to keep grains low.

Keep to protein salads in the evening.

THURSDAY

Exercise before breakfast.

Eat protein and fibre shake.

Eat protein and fibrous vegetables only – all day.

Drink plenty of water.

Allow some additional carbs either in the day or in the evening meal – you can make the choice.

FRIDAY

Exercise – a lighter session – preferably before breakfast.

Eat protein and fibre shake

Eat protein and fibrous vegetables only – all day.

Drink plenty of water.

Exercise again at night then eat a protein salad meal

To help you on your journey this book also features handy hints such as how to stone an avocado and useful information pages about the benefits of certain teas, dressings and spices.

Most ingredients can be bought from your supermarket, local health food store or online.

REMEMBER THESE HEALTHY EATING PRINCIPLES

> IF IT'S GREEN AND GROWS ABOVE THE GROUND EAT IT.

> IF IT RUNS, SWIM OR FLIES OR COMES FROM SOMETHING THAT DOES THOSE THINGS (EGGS), EAT IT.

> AVOID ANYTHING BROWN OR WHITE UNLESS YOU'VE EARNED IT.

> IF YOU'RE EATING AS ABOVE YOU CAN EAT WHAT YOU WANT ON THE WEEKENDS, USE THE PALMS FOR PORTIONS GUIDELINES FOR THE BODY WEIGHT YOU WANT.

> NEVER DRINK CALORIES – THAT MEANS NO FRUIT JUICE OR SOFT DRINKS IF FAT WEIGHT LOSS IS YOUR PRIMARY GOAL.

> EXERCISE FOR A LITTLE BIT EACH DAY.

> SLEEP PROPERLY.

RECIPE CONTENTS*

<BREAKFAST>

FROM TODAY, ALL YOUR BREAKFASTS WILL BE GEARED TO GETTING LEANER AND ADDING MORE MUSCLE, ALL DAY LONG.

TRY TO EAT WITHIN 45 MINUTES OF WAKING OR BEFORE 10AM IF EXERCISING ON AN EMPTY STOMACH.

<BREAKFAST>

POWER PORRIDGE WITH BLUEBERRIES AND PROTEIN POWDER*

<SERVES: 01>

<NUTRITION:>

PER SERVING WITHOUT YOGHURT:

> 500 KCAL

> 39G PROTEIN

> 65G CARBOHYDRATE

> 15G FAT

<INGREDIENTS:>

> 40-50G PORRIDGE OATS

> WATER/GOAT'S MILK, TO COVER THE OATS BY ½

> 1 SCOOP VANILLA (OR STRAWBERRY) WHEY PROTEIN POWDER

> 100G FROZEN BLUEBERRIES

> 1 SMALL HANDFUL RAISINS

> 1 HANDFUL PUMPKIN SEEDS/LINSEEDS

> 1 TSP CINNAMON

> 100G YOGHURT

<METHOD:>

In a pan cover the oats by as much again milk or water. Put on low heat and stir until the oats begin to thicken and take on the fluid.

When nearly fully cooked and becoming thicker, add the protein powder and remove from the heat.

Stir until the mixture thickens – be quick to avoid the protein denaturing and splitting.

Add the remaining ingredients to serve.

<BREAKFAST>

HOME-MADE MUESLI*

<SERVES: 02>

<NUTRITION:>

PER SERVING:

> 575 KCAL

> 31G PROTEIN

> 68G CARBOHYDRATE

> 21G FAT

" *I GOT THIS RECIPE FROM MY DAD, HE USED TO MAKE HOME-MADE MUESLI AND SELL IT AT COLLEGE – AHEAD OF HIS TIME I RECKON ON THAT ONE. I STILL MIGHT BRING IT OUT AS A SPECIALIST MUESLI. SOAKING THIS MIX OVERNIGHT HELPS BREAK DOWN SOME OF THE STARCHES AND ASSISTS WITH DIGESTION.*

<INGREDIENTS:>

> ½ APPLE, GRATED

> 1 DSP 0% FAT YOGHURT

> ½ SCOOP VANILLA WHEY PROTEIN POWDER (OR A FEW DROPS VANILLA EXTRACT WITH 2 EGG WHITES)

> 50G JUMBO OATS, SOAKED OVERNIGHT IN WATER

> 1 TBSP PUMPKIN SEEDS

> 1 TBSP MIXED NUTS

> 1 TBSP MIXED DRIED FRUIT

> 1 PINCH CINNAMON

"IF USING YOGHURT AND EGG WHITES RATHER THAN WHEY, STIR THEM TOGETHER UNTIL THE EGG WHITES BREAK DOWN."
<MATT LOVELL>

<METHOD:>

Add all the ingredients, mix and serve.

ALTERNATIVES:

This makes the base of an excellent, high-carb refuelling snack – just add honey and coconut oil half a cup of each.

Bind the mixture together spread thinly on a baking sheet, and cook in the top of a hot oven 190ºC for 10-15 minutes to make your own crunchy snack.

<BREAKFAST>

SPELT BREAD*

<MAKES 20 SLICES>

YOU NEED A BREAD MAKER FOR THIS ONE; I USE A WHOLEWHEAT RAPID BAKE PROGRAMME. THIS RECIPE MAKES A VERY NUTRITIOUS HIGH PROTEIN VEHICLE FOR ALL THE DIPS, SAUCES, EGGS OR BEANS OR WHATEVER YOU FANCY ON TOP. ALTHOUGH IT COMES OUT OF THE BREADMAKER LIKE A BRICK, IT'S GREAT TOASTED AND IS ACE WITH SOME MARMITE AND A COFFEE IN THE MORNING.

<NUTRITION:>

PER 45G SLICE:

> 115 KCAL

> 6G PROTEIN

> 14G CARBOHYDRATE

> 3G FAT

<INGREDIENTS:>

> 75G WHOLEGRAIN SPELT FLOUR

> 1 SACHET FAST ACTION YEAST

> 1 TSP SALT

> 1 TSP SUGAR

> ½ TSP VITAMIN C POWDER

> 1 HANDFUL RASINS

> 1 HANDFUL NUTS (WALNUTS, PUMPKIN OR LINSEEDS)

> 2 EGGS

> 2 TBSP OLIVE OIL

> 360ML WATER

<METHOD:>

Add all ingredients to a breadmaker and follow manufacturers instructions. Don't worry if the bread doesn't rise much its quite normal and still tastes good!

"YOU CAN ALSO ADD HERBS TO MAKE A NICE CHANGE, BUT THE QUALITY OF THE BREAD DEPENDS ON THE INGREDIENTS YOU USE."
<MATT LOVELL>

BEANS AND EGGS ON TOAST*

<SERVES: 02>

<NUTRITION:>

PER SERVING:

> 352 KCAL

> 22G PROTEIN

> 32G CARBOHYDRATE

> 14G FAT

THIS RECIPE REALLY SHOWS HOW THE INGREDIENTS CHANGE THE NUTRITIONAL VALUE OF A BASIC BRITISH CLASSIC.

<INGREDIENTS:>

> 2 EGGS

> 1 SPLASH VINEGAR

> 2 SLICES HOME-MADE SPELT BREAD (SEE PAGE 24)

> 1 X 200G CAN ORGANIC BAKED BEANS

> COCONUT OIL (OR GOAT'S BUTTER), TO TASTE

<METHOD:>

Add a splash of vinegar to a small pan of boiling water, crack the eggs straight into the pan. Cook for 3-4 minutes and remove when the egg white is solid.

Cook the toast and beans as desired. Butter the toast and serve with the egg and beans.

"AWESOME, WHOLESOME AND THEN SOME! GREAT FOR A SNACK OR BREAKFAST."
<MATT LOVELL>

SCRAMBLED EGGS AND SMOKED SALMON ON TOAST*

<SERVES: 01>

<NUTRITION:>

PER SERVING:

> 330 KCAL

> 40G PROTEIN

> 12G CARBOHYDRATE

> 14G FAT

 **PROTEIN BREAKFASTS ARE NOT ACTUALLY THAT DIFFICULT TO COOK IT'S JUST WE'RE ALL TOO LAZY AND STUCK IN OUR WAYS TO THINK OUT OF THE BOX. THIS DISH WITH IT'S HIGH OMEGA-3 CONTENT AND EXCELLENT SOURCES OF PROTEIN SETS YOU UP FOR A PROPER DAY'S WORK.**

<INGREDIENTS:>

> 2 EGGS

> COCONUT OIL, FOR FRYING

> 100G SMOKED SALMON

> SALT AND BLACK PEPPER, TO TASTE

> 1 SLICE HOME-MADE SPELT BREAD
   (SEE PAGE 24)

> LEMON JUICE, TO TASTE

<METHOD:>

Beat the eggs with a fork until the yolk and white are completely together. Add to a pan with a little butter.

Stir without letting the egg stick and remove just before the eggs sets, it should be hot through but still a little soft.

Meanwhile toast the bread and stir in flakes of salmon into the cooked eggs before seasoning.

Squeeze lemon juice over the top and serve.

"HAVING THIS WITHOUT THE TOAST MAKES THIS DISH INTO A LOW-CARB GREEN RECIPE."
<MATT LOVELL>

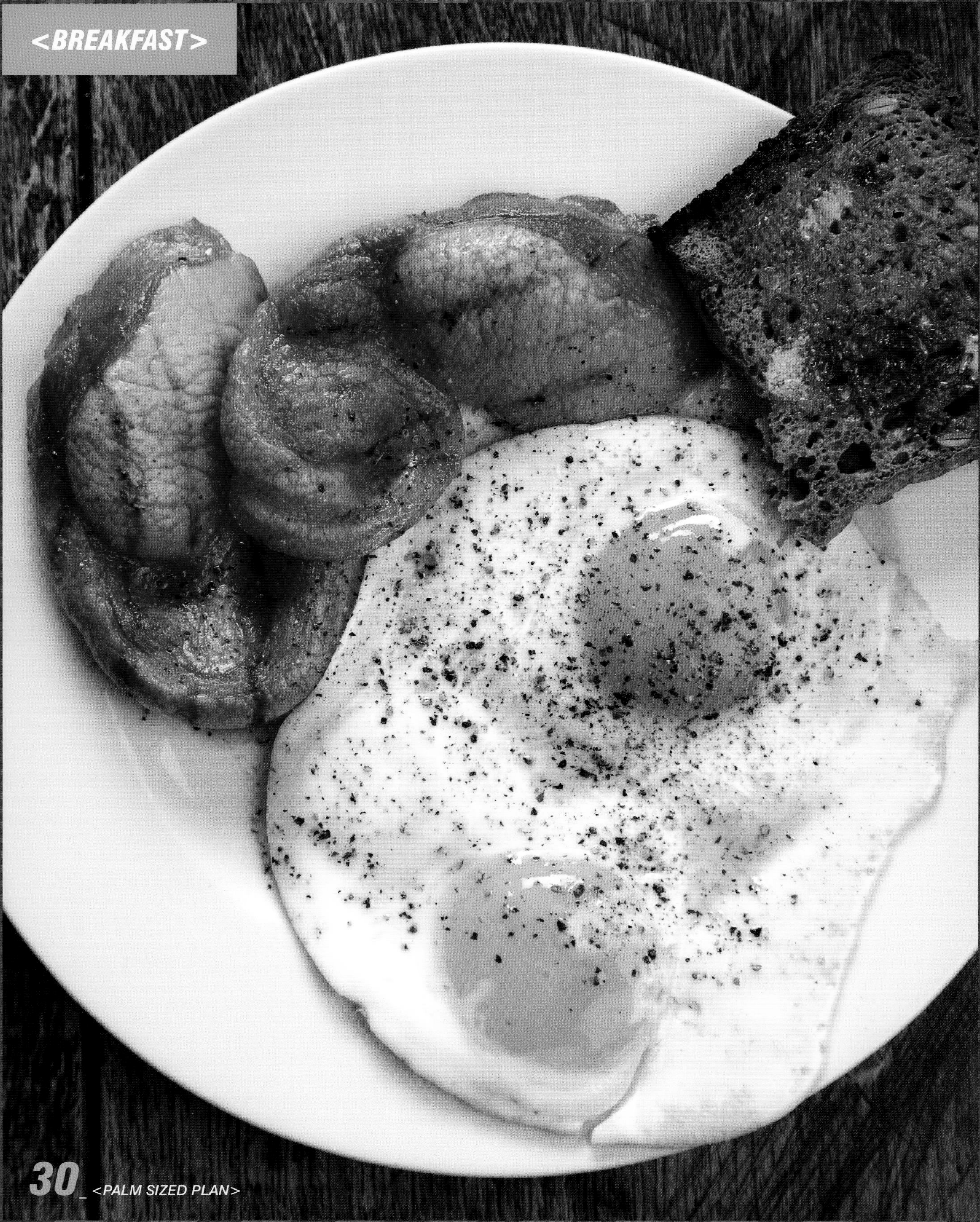

HEALTHY BACON AND EGGS*

<SERVES: 01>

<NUTRITION:>

PER SERVING:

> 280 KCAL

> 35G PROTEIN

> 2G CARBOHYDRATE

> 15G FAT

I USE THIS ONE IF I'M CUTTING CARBS DOWN TO DROP MY BODY FAT. IT'S REALLY DELICIOUS AND KEEPS ME FULL FOR A WHILE AFTERWARDS – IT PAYS TO GET THE BEST INGREDIENTS AS ALWAYS. SOMETIMES I'LL ADD A DROP OF TABASCO OR HARISSA PASTE.

<INGREDIENTS:>

> 2 LEAN BACON RASHERS, FAT TRIMMED

> 2 VINE TOMATOES

> 2 EGGS

> COCONUT OIL, TO GREASE

> 1 SLICE HOME-MADE SPELT BREAD, TOASTED (SEE PAGE 24)

> SALT AND PEPPER, TO TASTE

> PAPRIKA, TO TASTE

<METHOD:>

Grill the bacon on a medium heat until opaque.

Halve the tomatoes, salt and grill on a medium heat until slightly blackened.

For fried eggs, grease the pan like a baking tray with the minimum amount of coconut oil possible and fry as desired.

Serve with the toast and season to taste with the sea salt, black pepper and paprika.

ALTERNATIVES:

For scrambled eggs, scramble the eggs with 1 egg white, a teaspoon of dijon mustard and a splash of whole milk and grease a pan with coconut oil.

Cook on a medium heat until cooked through.

"HAVING THE BREAD WITH THIS MEAL MAKES IT PINK, SO TRY AND STAY WITHOUT FOR A TASTY GREEN MEAL."
<MATT LOVELL>

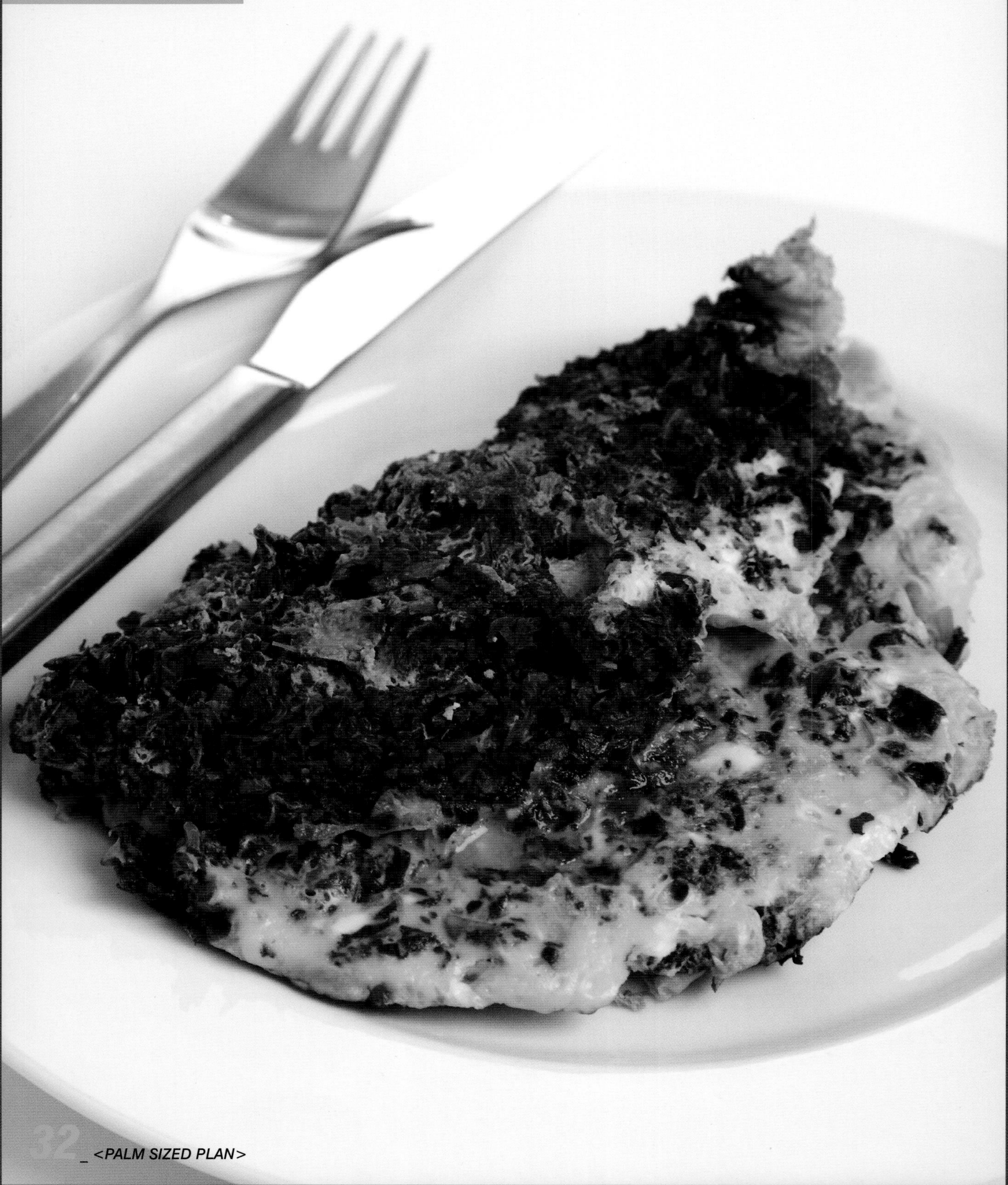

THREE EGG SPINACH OMELETTE*

<SERVES: 01>

EGGS ARE AN EXCELLENT SOURCE OF HIGH QUALITY PROTEINS AND NUTRIENTS. DON'T WORRY ABOUT THE CHOLESTEROL – FOR ACTIVE INDIVIDUALS EATING AN AVERAGE OF TWO EGGS PER DAY SHOULD POSE NO THREAT TO RAISED CHOLESTEROL LEVELS. IN FACT, A HIGH SUGAR AND CONSEQUENTIAL INSULIN PROFILE IS WORSE FOR YOUR CHOLESTEROL LEVELS AND SHOULD BE TACKLED FIRST.

<NUTRITION:>

PER SERVING:

> 295 KCAL

> 25G PROTEIN

> 1G CARBOHYDRATE

> 20G FAT

<INGREDIENTS:>

> 100G FROZEN SPINACH CUBES

> WATER, AS NEEDED

> COCONUT OIL, FOR FRYING

> 3 EGGS, BEATEN

<METHOD:>

Defrost the spinach cubes in the pan on a low heat with a small amount of water and coconut oil.

When the spinach is cooked make sure there is no residual water left, and then add the eggs.

Stir the eggs and spinach together to spread evenly. Cook over a low heat until opaque throughout.

<BREAKFAST>

TUNA AND CHILLI FRITTATA*

<SERVES: 01>

<NUTRITION:>

PER SERVING:

> 650 KCAL

> 60G PROTEIN

> 0G CARBOHYDRATE

> 45G FAT

> OMEGA EGGS ARE A DECENT WAY TO INCREASE YOUR OMEGA-3 FATTY ACID INTAKE. NORMAL EGGS ARE ALSO A VERY NUTRIENT DENSE FOOD. THIS OMELETTE COMES IN WITH A HIGH-PROTEIN AND LOW-CARB CONTENT, MAKING IT A PERFECT FILLING SNACK OR MEAL.

<INGREDIENTS:>

> 1 LARGE CHILLI, CHOPPED

> 1 GARLIC CLOVE, CHOPPED

> COCONUT OIL, AS NEEDED

> 1 X 185G TIN ALBACORE TUNA, DRAINED

> 3 EGGS

<METHOD:>

Fry the chilli and garlic in the coconut oil with the tuna.

Beat the eggs with a fork in a bowl until the yolks are well mixed with the whites.

Add the eggs to the tuna mixture and cook slowly over a medium heat, taking care not to burn the eggs.

"OTHER INGREDIENTS CAN BE ADDED TO INCREASE THE PORTION SIZE, SUCH AS ONIONS AND PEPPERS"
<MATT LOVELL>

<BREAKFAST>

CHORIZO EGGS*

<SERVES: 01>

<NUTRITION:>

PER SERVING:

> 530 KCAL

> 32G PROTEIN

> 23G CARBOHYDRATE

> 34G FAT

> *A HIGH PROTEIN, LOW CARBOHYDRATE BREAKFAST WHICH PACKS A SPICY PUNCH IF YOU CHOOSE THE RIGHT CHORIZO. KEEPS YOU FULL FOR A GOOD WHILE AFTERWARDS.*

<INGREDIENTS:>

> 50G CHORIZO, SLICED

> 2 EGGS

> SALT AND PEPPER, TO TASTE

> FRESH HERBS, TO TASTE

<METHOD:>

Pan-fry the chorizo in a dry pan, when caramelised add the eggs and cook to your liking.

Season with salt and pepper. Sprinkle with herbs if desired.

<BREAKFAST>

PROTEIN PANCAKES*

<SERVES: 02>

❝ **MOST PEOPLE THINK OF PANCAKES AS AN UNHEALTHY FOOD AND THEY'D BE RIGHT FOR THE COMMERCIALLY AVAILABLE MIXES, BUT IF YOU RECONSIDER THE INGREDIENTS SUCH AS FLOUR, EGGS, MILK AND PROTEIN POWDER, YOU CAN MAKE LOW-CARB, HIGH FIBRE PATTIES – PLUS KIDS LOVE THEM TOO.**

<NUTRITION:>

PER SERVING:

> 150 KCAL

> 13G PROTEIN

> 6G CARBOHYDRATE

> 8G FAT

<INGREDIENTS:>

> 25G PUMPKIN SEEDS (LINSEEDS OR OTHER NUTS CAN ALSO BE USED)

> 1 EGG

> 2 SCOOPS UNFLAVOURED WHEY PROTEIN POWDER

> 1 SMALL SPLASH GOAT'S MILK

> COCONUT OIL, AS NEEDED

> 1 TSP MANUKA HONEY

<METHOD:>

To make the flour grind the seeds/nuts in a coffee grinder until smooth. Combine with the egg and protein powder and add a small splash of goat's milk.

Add more goat's milk to the mixture 2 teaspoons at a time until the mixture is the consistency of thick batter.

Melt a good amount of coconut oil in the pan and heat over a medium/high heat.

Move the mixture and fold with a spatula – similar to cooking an omelette. Leave for 2-3 minutes per pancake until solid all the way through and easily detachable around the edge.

Flip, cook the other side and dress with the honey as desired.

<BREAKFAST>

BROCCOLI AND BURGERS FOR BREAKFAST*

<SERVES: 04>

" STARTING THE DAY WITH MEAT AND VEGETABLES OR MEAT AND NUTS IS A VERY MALE ENERGY OR 'YANG' BREAKFAST – WITH PORK BEING ONE OF THE MOST YANG FOODS IN CHINESE MEDICINE. ALL MEATS ARE HIGH IN TYROSINE AND OTHER AMINOS WHICH HELP WAKE THE MIND UP, NOURISH THE IMMUNE SYSTEM AND AVOID REBOUND HYPOGLYCEMIA WHICH OCCURS WHEN WE EAT SIMPLE FAST RELEASE HIGH GI CEREALS.

<NUTRITION:>

PER SERVING:

> 465 KCAL

> 39G PROTEIN

> 6G CARBOHYDRATE

> 31G FAT

<INGREDIENTS:>

> 500G ORGANIC LEAN STEAK MINCE

> 1 EGG YOLK

> 2 DSP PESTO

> 1 TSP CAJUN SPICES

> 1 GARLIC CLOVE, FINELY CHOPPED

> SALT AND PEPPER, TO TASTE

> SEED FLOUR (SESAME SEED FLOUR, LINSEED FLOUR, OR SPELT FLOUR) TO BIND

> 800G BROCCOLI

> PESTO, TO SERVE

<METHOD:>

Combine all ingredients but the broccoli and mix together with your hands. Add enough seed flour (sesame seed flour, linseed flour, or spelt flour) to dry out mixture and stop it sticking.

Form into patties. Grill for 8 minutes on a high heat.

Steam the broccoli for 5 minutes and serve with the burgers with a little pesto dressing.

<BREAKFAST>

BLUEBERRIES AND YOGHURT *

< SERVES: 01 >

< NUTRITION: >

PER SERVING:

> 230 KCAL

> 16G PROTEIN

> 40G CARBOHYDRATE

> 01G FAT

POWER-PACKED BERRIES SCORE HIGHLY ON THE ORAC SCALE (A SCALE WHICH MEASURES THE AMOUNT OF A FOOD THAT PROTECTS CELLS AGAINST DAMAGE) – AND THE 0% GREEK YOGHURT IS HIGH IN PROTEIN AND CONTAINS ZERO FAT. IT'S AN EXCELLENT RECOVERY MEAL AND IS ALSO LOW ENOUGH IN ENERGY TO MAKE A PERFECT END TO A MEAL – ALL GOOD.

< INGREDIENTS: >

> 1 X 170G POT 0% GREEK YOGHURT

> 60G BLUEBERRIES

< METHOD: >

Combine the yoghurt and blueberries together and serve.

"WASH THE BLUEBERRIES IF BOUGHT FROM A SUPERMARKET. IDEALLY GROW YOUR OWN – A COUPLE OF BLUEBERRY PLANTS IN POTS CAN SEE YOU RIGHT FOR EIGHT LARGE BOWLS OF BERRIES"
< MATT LOVELL >

<LUNCH>

THESE LIGHT LUNCHES ARE A GREAT WAY TO KEEP YOU GOING THROUGHOUT THE AFTERNOON, AND YOU CAN COMPLEMENT

THEM WITH A SMOOTHIE IF YOU FEEL A DIP LATER IN THE DAY. JUST TRY AND KEEP TO YOUR PORTION SIZES.

<LUNCH>

HUMOUS*

<SERVES: 2 AS A MEAL, 4 FOR A SNACK>

<NUTRITION:>

PER 70G SERVING:

> 170 KCAL

> 6G PROTEIN

> 10G CARBOHYDRATE

> 12G FAT

BEANS AND PULSES SUPPLY A GOOD SOURCE OF PROTEIN AND FIBRE – THE TEXTURE OF THESE DIPS CAN BE ALTERED WITH MORE OR LESS TAHINI OR OLIVE OIL DEPENDING ON YOUR PREFERENCES AND FITNESS REQUIREMENTS FROM THIS MEAL. COMBINING BEANS AND PULSES WITH GRAINS MAKES A COMPLETE PROTEIN MEAL.

<INGREDIENTS:>

> 2 DSP SESAME SEEDS/TAHINI

> 1 GARLIC CLOVE

> 1 X 440G CAN CHICKPEAS

> 3 TBSP OLIVE OIL

> JUICE OF ½ LEMON

> 1 LARGE PINCH SALT

> 1 PINCH PAPRIKA

"AS A SNACK THIS MEAL BECOMES GREEN."
<MATT LOVELL>

<METHOD:>

Add all the ingredients to a blender and pulse until smooth but with a firm consistency.

Serve with oatcakes, rice cakes, rye thins, wholewheat crackers or crudités.

ALTERNATIVE:

For a kidney bean humous variation, replace the chickpeas with kidney beans and add a pinch of chilli, powdered or freshly chopped, to serve.

<LUNCH>

BRUSSELS SPROUTS AND CHESTNUTS*

<SERVES: 04>

<NUTRITION:>

PER SERVING:

> 102 KCAL

> 6G PROTEIN

> 22G CARBOHYDRATE

> 11G FAT

 **IF YOU'VE BEEN FORAGING FOR FREE FOOD IN YOUR LOCAL PARK OR WOOD YOU WILL NEED THE SAME UNPREPARED WEIGHT QUANTITY OF THE CHESTNUTS AS THE SPROUTS. TO PREPARE THEM NICK EACH SHELL AND BOIL THEM IN WATER FOR 4 MINUTES, THEN TAKE THEM OUT OF THE WATER ONE AT A TIME TO SHELL, AS THEY'RE EASIER TO DO THAT WAY OR JUST BUY THEM PREPARED.**

<INGREDIENTS:>

> 2 TBSP COCONUT OIL

> 500G BRUSSELS SPROUTS, PREPARED

> 150G PANCETTA CUBES

> 250G CHESTNUTS, PREPARED

> SALT AND PEPPER, TO TASTE

<METHOD:>

Generally a good rule of thumb is to keep the prepared brussels sprouts double to the prepared chestnut quantity. Heat the fat in a large skillet or frying pan over a moderate heat, the aim being to have enough space for all the sprouts to touch the base of the pan, then add the brussels and brown them, turning regularly so that they are golden brown all over.

Then add the pancetta cubes and cook for around 5 minutes until crispy before adding the prepared chestnuts, gently mixing them in, letting them heat through until piping hot.

Season to taste.

THREE BEAN SALAD*

<SERVES: 03>

<NUTRITION:>

PER SERVING:

> 185 KCAL

> 8G PROTEIN

> 27G CARBOHYDRATE

> 5G FAT

MIXED BEAN SALAD CAN BE EATEN ALONE AS A QUICK SNACK OR SERVED WITH THE QUICHE RECIPE TO MAKE A ROUNDED MEAL. IT'S AN EASY DISH TO PREPARE AND CONTAINS HEAPS OF SOLUBLE FIBRE AND PROTEINS – THIS DISH IS ALSO VERY LOW GI MAKING IT ONE WHICH CAN KEEP YOU SUSTAINED FOR SEVERAL HOURS AFTERWARDS.

<INGREDIENTS:>

> 1 X 100G CAN BORLOTTI BEANS

> 1 X 100G CAN KIDNEY BEANS

> 1 X 100G CAN GIANT BUTTER BEANS

> 50G VACUUM-PACKED CHESTNUTS, CHOPPED

> 1 TBSP HOME-MADE KETCHUP

> 1 TBSP BALSAMIC VINEGAR

> 1 TBSP EXTRA VIRGIN OLIVE OIL

> 1 TSP DIJON MUSTARD

<METHOD:>

Drain the beans and mix together with the chopped chestnuts.

Mix together the home-made ketchup, balsamic vinegar, extra virgin olive oil and the Dijon mustard and drizzle over the beans and serve.

<LUNCH>

BORSCHT SOUP*

<SERVES: 04>

<NUTRITION:>

PER SERVING:

> 210 KCAL

> 6G PROTEIN

> 18G CARBOHYDRATE

> 13G FAT

> **BORSCHT – THIS BEETROOT BASED SOUP IS GREAT FOR PEOPLE WITH HIGH BLOOD PRESSURE AS THE HIGH NITRATE CONTENT OF BEETS ACTS TO INCREASE BLOOD FLOW THROUGH A VASODILATION EFFECT, EXPANDING THE BLOOD VESSELS! THIS ALSO MEANS IT CAN HELP MAKE EXERCISE MORE EFFICIENT AS IT HELPS MORE OXYGEN TO REACH THE WORKING MUSCLES. BEETS ALSO HELP LIVER AND GALLBLADDER FUNCTION.**

<INGREDIENTS:>

> 1 LITRE LAMB (OR DUCK) STOCK

> 455G FRESH BEETROOT, GRATED

> 2 TBSP RED WINE VINEGAR

> 2 TBSP TOMATO CONCENTRATE

> 227G ROOT VEGETABLES, SHREDDED

> 455G CABBAGE, SHREDDED

> 2 TBSP COCONUT OIL

> 1 TBSP BUTTER

> ½ TBSP FLOUR

> SALT, PEPPER AND SUGAR, TO TASTE

> CHIVES, TO SERVE

<METHOD:>

To a quarter of a litre of stock add the grated beetroot – reserving 3 tablespoons to add later.

To this add the red wine vinegar and tomato concentrate, cover and simmer for 1 hour over a medium heat, being careful not to boil

Fry the root vegetables and cabbage in oil until lightly golden, the key being to cook them as quickly as possible keeping them fresh flavoured.

When the vegetables are cooked add them all into the pan of cooking beetroot stock along with the 3 tablespoons of reserved shredded beetroot and simmer for 5 minutes.

To thicken the soup mash together the flour and butter to make a paste and slowly add to the stock mix, stirring continuously.

Finally season the soup with the salt, pepper and sugar (or honey) and add few chopped chives to serve.

"IF YOU NEED TO USE A BEEF STOCK CUBE USE IT AT A WEAKER DILUTION THAN RECOMMENDED"
<MATT LOVELL>

MISO SOUP*

<SERVES: 04>

<NUTRITION:>

PER SERVING:

> 245 KCAL

> 27G PROTEIN

> 76G CARBOHYDRATE

> 18G FAT

" LEAVING OUT THE NOODLES AND POACHING TWO EGGS INSTEAD OF ONE BRINGS UP THE PROTEIN CONTENT AND REALLY CUTS THE CARBS DOWN LOW. THIS SOUP IS ALSO AN EXCELLENT WAY TO REHYDRATE DUE TO ITS HIGH MINERAL AND ELECTROLYTE CONTENT.

<INGREDIENTS:>

> 1 TBSP SHREDDED NORI (OR WAKAME SEAWEED)

> 1½ LITRES PRE-MADE VEGETABLE (OR CHICKEN) STOCK

> 35G FERMENTED ORGANIC MISO

> 4 EGG NOODLE NESTS

> 1 BLOCK FIRM SILKEN TOFU, CUT INTO 2½ CM CUBES (OR 1 EGG)

> ½ TSP SESAME OIL

> 3 SPRING ONIONS, CHOPPED

> 4 EGGS

> 1 DASH SOY SAUCE, TO SERVE

<METHOD:>

Boil the seaweed in the stock for 5-10 minutes over a high heat then mix in the miso.

Add all the remaining ingredients but the egg or soy sauce and simmer. If using the egg add after 5 minutes and simmer for another 5 minutes. If using tofu continue cooking for the full 10 minutes.

Season with the soy sauce and serve.

<LUNCH>

HEALTHY BAKED JACKET POTATO AND SALMON MAYONNAISE*

<SERVES: 02>

 **SOMETIMES THE SIMPLEST DISHES CAN BE THE MOST NUTRITIOUS AND DELICIOUS. THESE PURPLE MAJESTY POTATOES ARE AWESOME WITH THEIR ADDED ANTIOXIDANT BONUS WHICH HAS A NUMBER OF BENEFICIAL HEALTH BENEFITS, PLUS THEY TASTE JUST LIKE NORMAL POTATOES. ADDING SOME SALMON WITH A LITTLE MAYONNAISE AND A DECENT SALAD MAKES THIS A PERFECT RECOVERY MEAL OR MEAL TO UP YOUR CARBOHYDRATE RESERVES BEFORE TRAINING.**

<NUTRITION:>

PER SERVING:

> 360 KCAL

> 23G PROTEIN

> 43G CARBOHYDRATE

> 11G FAT

<INGREDIENTS:>

> 2 MEDIUM PURPLE MAJESTY POTATOES

> 1 X 225G TIN WILD ALASKAN SALMON

> 1 DSP LOW-FAT MAYONNAISE

> 1 X 145G BAG OF ROCKET AND WATERCRESS (OR STANDARD MIXED LEAVES)

> 1 DSP OLIVE OIL

> 1 DSP CIDER VINEGAR

> 1 DSP DIJON MUSTARD

<METHOD:>

Preheat the oven to 180ºC. Wrap the potatoes in foil and bake for approximately 40 minutes or until cooked.

Mix the olive oil, cider vinegar and Dijon mustard together and then dress the salad leaves.

Mix the salmon with the mayonnaise and serve together with the potato and the green leafy salad.

<LUNCH>

SARDINES ON TOAST*

<SERVES: 01>

" SARDINES CONTAIN GOOD PROTEIN, MASSIVE LEVELS OF OMEGA-3, BIO AVAILABLE CALCIUM AND DECENT LEVELS OF VITAMIN D TOO – SO ALL IN ALL THEY STILL ARE A LITTLE POWERHOUSE OF PROTEIN-PACKED GOODNESS (JUST DON'T EAT THEM IN A CROWDED OFFICE).

<NUTRITION:>

PER SERVING:

> 280 KCAL

> 25G PROTEIN

> 16G CARBOHYDRATE

> 13G FAT

<INGREDIENTS:>

> 1 SLICE HOME-MADE SPELT BREAD
  (PAGE 24)

> 1 X 120G CAN SARDINES

> LEMON JUICE, TO TASTE

> PEPPER, TO TASTE

<METHOD:>

Toast the bread as desired then spread the sardines on top.

Squeeze lemon juice and sprinkle pepper over and enjoy.

<LUNCH>

CLUB
SANDWICH*

<SERVES: 02>

THE PROTEIN-RICH SANDWICH HAS AN ENDLESS STREAM OF POSSIBLE FILLINGS. MAKE IT AN OPEN SANDWICH TO INCREASE THE PROTEIN AND VEGETABLE RATIO, OR JUST STICK TO THE 'SCOOBY SNACK' STYLE WHERE THE FILLINGS ARE OF GREATER VOLUME THAN THE BREAD. KEEP TO HOME-MADE BREADS AND QUALITY FILLINGS FOR A POWER PACKED SNACK.

<NUTRITION:>

PER SERVING:

> 600 KCAL

> 75G PROTEIN

> 45G CARBOHYDRATE

> 13G FAT

<INGREDIENTS:>

> 2 ANCHOVY FILLETS

> 1 TSP DIJON MUSTARD

> 1 DSP LOW-FAT MAYONNAISE

> 4 SLICES HOME-MADE SPELT BREAD
  (SEE PAGE 24)

> 1 CHICKEN BREAST, COOKED AND SLICED

> 2 SLICES LEAN GAMMON

> ½ AVOCADO, MASHED

> 125G MOZZARELLA, SLICED

> 8 CHERRY TOMATOES

> 2 DSP PICKLE

> ROCKET LEAVES, TO SERVE

<METHOD:>

Mash the anchovy fillets with the mustard and mayonnaise and spread on the bread.

Stack the other ingredients in the desired order, top with the rocket leaves and serve.

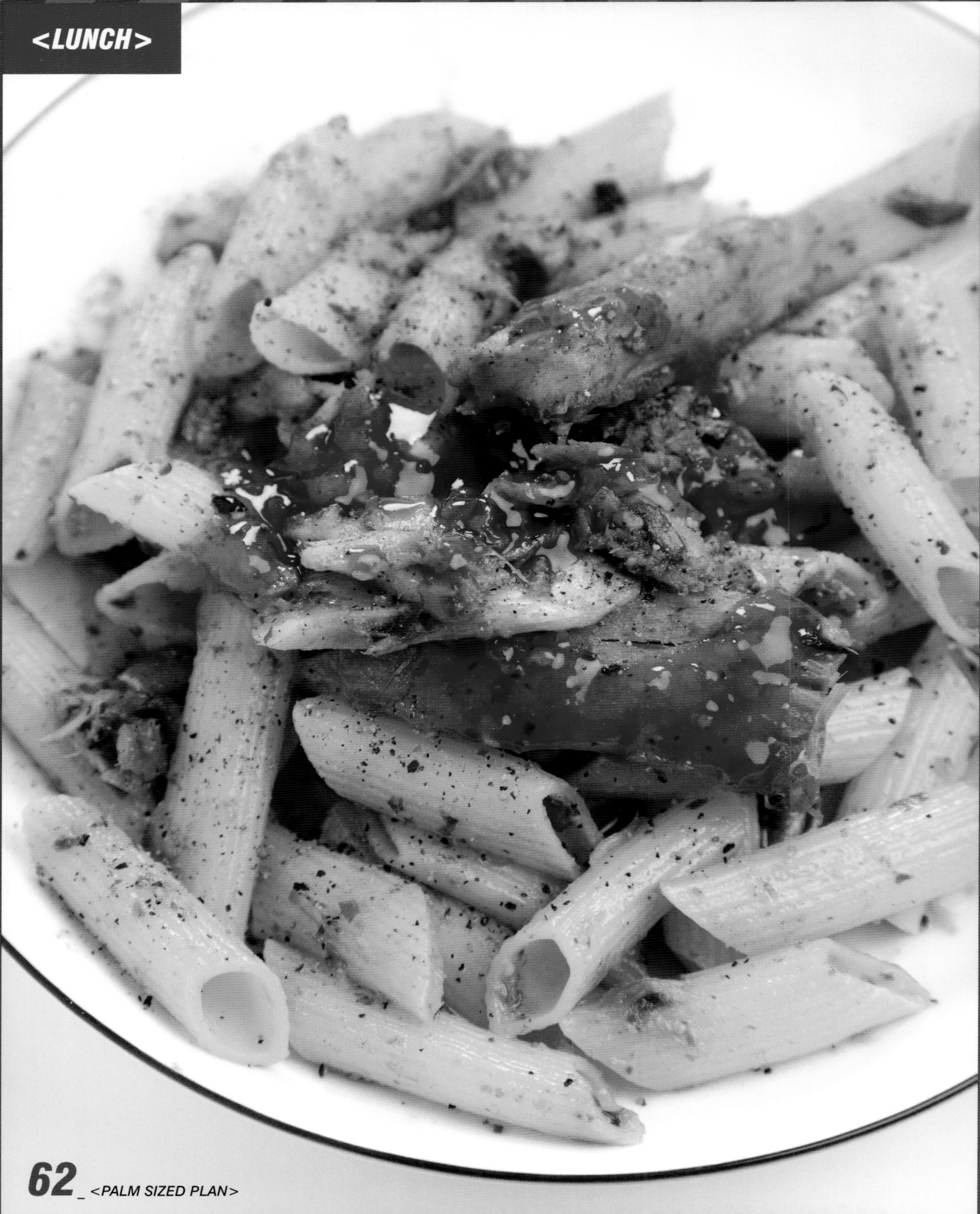

TUNA GARLIC PASTA*

<SERVES: 02>

" THIS IS AN OLD FAVOURITE OF MINE WHICH I'VE BEEN MAKING FOR YEARS AS AN OFF-PLAN HIGH CALORIE FEED UP. IT'S STILL PRETTY GOOD WITH PLENTY OF GARLIC, CHILLI AND ALBACORE TUNA PROTEIN GOODNESS – AND YOU CAN USE WHEAT-FREE PENNE IF YOU NEED TO.

<NUTRITION:>

PER SERVING:

> 450 KCAL

> 45G PROTEIN

> 60G CARBOHYDRATE

> 4G FAT

<INGREDIENTS:>

> 1 TSP OLIVE OIL

> 2 TSP CRUSHED GARLIC

> 4 FRESH CHILLI, CHOPPED WITH SEEDS

> 1 X 400G TIN ALBACORE TUNA, IN OLIVE OIL

> 500G PENNE PASTA

> 5 TSP FRESH BASIL, CHOPPED

> 2 DSP PESTO

> SWEET CHILLI SAUCE, TO TASTE

> MATURE CHEDDAR, GRATED

> BLACK PEPPER, TO TASTE

<METHOD:>

In a pan heat the olive oil over a low heat, then add the garlic and chilli and soften.

Add the tuna and cover with a lid, then cook over a low heat until it turns nice and crispy – if the mixture gets too dry add more oil.

Cook for as long as it takes for the tuna to go crispy around 5-10 minutes, stirring regularly and keeping the pan covered where possible.

Meanwhile cook the pasta as per the packet instructions. When cooked to your taste mix in the basil, pesto, chilli sauce and a little grated mature cheddar.

Season with pepper and serve with the tuna mix and a little chilli sauce.

<LUNCH>

SPICY BACON AND TOMATO PASTA*

<SERVES: 02>

 **A GREAT RECOVERY/CARB UP MEAL – WITH LOADS OF LYCOPENE GOODNESS FROM THE COOKED TOMATOES. COOKING THE TOMATOES AND COMBINING THEM WITH THE OLIVE OIL INCREASES THE ABSORPTION OF THIS VALUABLE NUTRIENT BY UP TO 70 PER CENT.**

<NUTRITION:>

PER SERVING:

> 550 KCAL

> 23G PROTEIN

> 45G CARBOHYDRATE

> 31G FAT

<INGREDIENTS:>

> OLIVE OIL, FOR FRYING

> 5 GARLIC CLOVES, CHOPPED

> 4 FRESH LARGE CHILLIS, WITH SEEDS

> 1 X 110G PACKET PANCETTA

> 1 X 440G TIN CHOPPED TOMATOES

> 2 BAY LEAVES

> 1 CHICKEN STOCK CUBE

> 90G PASTA

<METHOD:>

Fry the garlic, chilli and pancetta in the oil over a medium heat until crispy and slightly burnt.

Add the tomatoes, bay leaves and crumbled stock cube and simmer until the tomatoes begin to caramelise.

Cook the pasta following the packet instructions and stir into the sauce, then serve.

MACKEREL PATE*

<SERVES: 06>

<NUTRITION:>

PER SERVING:

> 170 KCAL

> 16G PROTEIN

> 3G CARBOHYDRATE

> 11G FAT

> A KING OF THE OILY FISH WORLD – MACKEREL COMES UP VERY HIGH IN OMEGA-3 CONTENT. ROLLMOPS ARE THE HIGHEST AVAILABLE SOURCE, PROBABLY BECAUSE THEY'VE NOT BEEN COOKED AND OMEGA-3 TENDS TO DECREASE WITH HEAT AND LIGHT EXPOSURE BEING VERY FRAGILE MOLECULES.

<INGREDIENTS:>

> 3 MACKEREL FILLETS

> 50G GREEK YOGHURT

> 1 DSP MILD GRAINY MUSTARD

> 1 DSP HORSERADISH

> ½ APPLE, PIPS INCLUDED

> SALT AND PEPPER, TO TASTE

> 1 TSP LEMON JUICE

> 1 GARLIC CLOVE

<METHOD:>

Put all the ingredients in a blender and pulse to maintain a firm consistency – be careful not to over blend into a soup!

Serve with oatcakes, rice cakes or whole-grain crackers.

<LUNCH>

BABAGANOUSH*

<SERVES: 04>

THIS AUBERGINE BASED DIP IS AN EXCELLENT WAY TO UP THE VEGETABLE COMPONENT OF A SNACK-BASED MEAL WHICH YOU WOULD EAT WITH OAT OR RICE CAKES. COLD MEATS AND HARD BOILED EGGS ROUND OFF THIS SNACK-TYPE APPROACH WELL.

<NUTRITION:>

PER 100G SERVING:

> 75 KCAL

> 3G PROTEIN

> 7G CARBOHYDRATE

> 4G FAT

<INGREDIENTS:>

> 1 x 400G CAN COOKED AUBERGINES, DRAINED OF JUICE/OIL

> 2 GARLIC CLOVES

> ½ TSP SALT

> 1 TBSP LEMON JUICE

> 1 TBSP TAHINI

> 1 LARGE PINCH GROUND CUMIN

> 1 PINCH GROUND WHITE PEPPER

> 2 HEAPED TBSP GREEK YOGHURT

> EXTRA VIRGIN OLIVE OIL AND CHOPPED FLAT LEAF PARSLEY OR CORIANDER, TO SERVE

<METHOD:>

Put all the ingredients in a blender and blitz until smooth.

Serve with oatcakes, rice cakes, rye thins, whole-grain crackers or crudités.

<LUNCH>

MIXED ANTIPASTO*

<SERVES: 01>

❝ ANOTHER QUICK AND NUTRITIOUS SNACK DISH GREAT FOR SUMMER EVENINGS – LOADED WITH HEALTHY VEGETABLES ALONG WITH PROTEIN AND ESSENTIAL FATTY ACIDS FROM THE PICKLED ANCHOVIES.

<NUTRITION:>

PER SERVING:

> 140 KCAL

> 7G PROTEIN

> 8G CARBOHYDRATE

> 9G FAT

<INGREDIENTS:>

> 25G SUN-DRIED TOMATOES

> 4 FILLETS PICKLED UNSALTED ANCHOVIES

> 40G MARINATED ARTICHOKES

> 40G MARINATED GRILLED VEGETABLES

<METHOD:>

Plate up as pictured or as desired.

"YOU CAN ENJOY THIS WITH A PIECE OF CRUSTY BREAD, BE AWARE THAT IT TURNS IT INTO A PINK DISH"
<MATT LOVELL>

<LUNCH>

TUNA ONION AND TOMATO SALAD WITH BORLOTTI BEANS*

<SERVES: 01>

❝ A SUMMER SPECIAL, THIS SALAD VIRTUALLY PREPARES ITSELF. IT OFFERS EXCELLENT NUTRIENTS FROM THE BEANS AND RAW ONIONS AND YOU CAN VARY THE DRESSINGS IF YOU EAT IT REGULARLY. YOU CAN ALSO ADD SOME FRESH BREAD OR OAT CAKES IF YOU NEED THE EXTRA ENERGY.

<NUTRITION:>

PER SERVING:

> 290 KCAL

> 28G PROTEIN

> 25G CARBOHYDRATE

> 9G FAT

<INGREDIENTS:>

> 1 X 225 CAN ALBACORE TUNA, IN OLIVE OIL

> 1 RED ONION, CHOPPED

> 8 CHERRY TOMATOES, HALVED

> 100G BORLOTTI BEANS

> 3 CAPFULS CIDER VINEGAR

> PEPPER, TO TASTE

<METHOD:>

Combine all the ingredients together and serve with a generous sprinkling of ground black pepper.

<LUNCH>

COMPLEX SALMON SALAD*

<SERVES: 01>

THE COMPLEX SALAD IS THE CORNER-STONE TO A HEALTHY DIET AND MAINTAINING LOW BODY FATS. YOU NEED AT LEAST 10 INGREDIENTS AND A CREATIVE MIND AROUND DRESSINGS. COMPLEX SALADS CAN BE CREATED FROM SCRATCH IN 10 MINUTES, MAKING THEM CONVENIENT AS WELL AS HEALTHY AND VERSATILE.

<NUTRITION:>

PER SERVING:

> 500 KCAL

> 45G PROTEIN

> 21G CARBOHYDRATE

> 26G FAT

<INGREDIENTS:>

> 1 X 100G FILLET WILD ALASKAN SALMON

> COCONUT OIL, AS NEEDED

> 1 GARLIC CLOVE

> ½ LEMON JUICE, FRESHLY SQUEEZED

> 100G BROCCOLI

> OLIVES, AS DESIRED

> CELERY, AS DESIRED

> 1 LARGE SPRIG DILL

> 1 DSP CAPERS

> 45G BISTRO-STYLE SALAD

> 30G BROAD BEANS

> 1 LARGE SPRIG PARSLEY

> 2 TSP OLIVE OIL

> 2 TSP HONEY

> 1 TSP CRUSHED GARLIC

> 2 TBSP CIDER VINEGAR

<METHOD:>

Pan fry the salmon in the coconut oil and cook for 3-4 minutes each side on a medium heat.

Chop the vegetables as desired.

For the dressing mix the olive oil, honey, crushed garlic and vinegar together.

Mix all the ingredients together in a bowl and pour over the dressing ingredients.

Toss the salad in the mixture and serve together with the salmon.

"THE DRESSING CAN BE MADE WITH MORE VINEGAR AND LESS OIL TO LOWER THE FAT CONTENT."
<MATT LOVELL>

CRAB SALAD*

<SERVES: 01>

A GEM OF A SALAD – CRUSTACEANS LIKE CRAB PROVIDE A USEFUL SOURCE OF ZINC, THE MINERAL REQUIRED FOR OPTIMUM TESTOSTERONE PRODUCTION, WITH AN 85G SERVING CONTAINING 6.5MG. OTHER INGREDIENTS INCLUDE BLOOD-THINNING CHILLI AND GARLIC ALONG WITH ONIONS AND ROCKET.

<NUTRITION:>

PER SERVING:

> 515 KCAL

> 43G PROTEIN

> 19G CARBOHYDRATE

> 29G FAT

<INGREDIENTS:>

> 20G PINE NUTS

> 200G FRESH CRAB MEAT (OR CANNED IF FRESH IS NOT AVAILABLE)

> ½ RED ONION, FINELY CHOPPED

> 1 GARLIC CLOVE, FINELY CHOPPED

> 2 LARGE CHILLIS, FINELY CHOPPED

> 1 TBSP RED WINE VINEGAR

> 1 TBSP TAMARI SOY SAUCE

> 1 TBSP OLIVE OIL

> 30G ROCKET

> 20G WATERCRESS

> 10 CHERRY TOMATOES, HALVED

> CORIANDER, TO SERVE

<METHOD:>

Lightly brown the pine nuts in a pan over a medium heat, taking care not to burn them.

Mix the crab with the onion, garlic and chilli.

Mix all the red wine vinegar, tamari soy sauce and olive oil together. Add to the crab mix and leave to infuse for around 20 minutes.

Mix the remaining salad ingredients together and then dress with the crab mixture. Add the coriander if desired.

"FRESH CRAB IS ALWAYS BETTER BUT INCREASES THE PREPARATION TIME SIGNIFICANTLY"
<MATT LOVELL>

HOW TO STONE AN AVOCADO*

<1> HOLD THE AVOCADO IN ONE HAND AND PIERCE THE FRUIT TO THE CENTRE.

<2> WHEN AGAINST THE STONE TURN THE FRUIT AROUND USING THE STONE AS A GUIDE – KEEPING THE BLADE AWAY FROM YOUR PALM.

<3> WHEN SCORED COMPLETLEY TWIST THE AVOCADO SEPARATING THE TWO PARTS.

<4> SCOOP OUT THE STONE AND DISCARD, THEN USE THE FLESH IN SALADS OR EAT STRAIGHT WITH A LITTLE DRESSING.

<LUNCH>

CRAB GUACAMOLE SALAD*

<SERVES: 02>

A GREAT AND ATTRACTIVE LOOKING EXAMPLE OF A PROTEIN SALAD. EXTREMELY QUICK TO PREPARE AND HIGHLY NUTRITIOUS. THE DRESSING MAKES ITSELF WITH A MIXTURE OF MUSTARD, GARLIC AND ORANGE JUICE.

<NUTRITION:>

PER SERVING:

> 250 KCAL

> 18G PROTEIN

> 12G CARBOHYDRATE

> 15G FAT

<INGREDIENTS:>

> 1 AVOCADO

> 125G FRESH CRAB

> SALT AND PEPPER, TO TASTE

> 1 ORANGE, SEGMENTED

> 1 TSP DIJON MUSTARD

> 1 HANDFUL RADICCHIO LEAVES

> 1 X 75G PACKET WATERCRESS

> 1 CHICORY HEAD

> ½ CUCUMBER, CHOPPED

> 5-6 CHERRY TOMATOES

> ½ RED PEPPER, CHOPPED

> 1 GARLIC CLOVE, CHOPPED

> 28G PRAWNS, COOKED

<METHOD:>

Remove the flesh from the avocado and pulse together with the crab and seasoning once or twice in a food processor until roughly chopped/halfway to purée.

Chop the orange and coat with the mustard — set aside.

Arrange the leaves, cucumber, orange, prawns, tomatoes, pepper and garlic. The juice from the orange and liquids released from blending should dress the salad. Add the crab mix on top and arrange prawns.

Season as desired and serve.

<LUNCH>

PRAWN COCKTAIL *

<SERVES: 02>

❝ THIS DELICIOUS MIX OF KING PRAWNS, SPICY SAUCE AND AVOCADO IS A STANDALONE MEAL OR DECENT STARTER. AVOCADOS ARE KNOWN FOR THEIR MANY HEALTH GIVING BENEFITS, ONE GREAT THING THEY DO IS TO INCREASE CAROTENOID UPTAKE – THE COLOURFUL HEALTHY STUFF IN VEGETABLES. THEY ARE ALSO KNOWN TO HAVE IMMUNE ENHANCING AND HEART PROTECTIVE EFFECTS.

<NUTRITION:>

PER SERVING:

> 310 KCAL

> 20G PROTEIN

> 8G CARBOHYDRATE

> 22G FAT

<INGREDIENTS:>

> 200G WILD ATLANTIC JUMBO PRAWNS

> 2 RED CHILLIES, CHOPPED AND DESEEDED

> 4 GARLIC CLOVES, CHOPPED

> 1 TBSP OLIVE OIL

> 3-4 TBSP LOW-FAT CREME FRAICHE

> 3-4 TBSP HOME-MADE KETCHUP

> 1 RIPE, ORGANIC HASS AVOCADO

> 1 X 200G PACKET ROCKET AND WATERCRESS

> 1 TSP SMOKED PAPRIKA

> SALT AND PEPPER, TO TASTE

<METHOD:>

Fry the prawns with the chopped chilli and garlic in the olive oil over a medium heat, until the prawns are pink throughout. You can also use any cooked prawns you like but try to make sure that they are wild Atlantic prawns if possible.

Combine the crème fraîche, ketchup and prawns, stone the avocado halves and spoon the prawn cocktail into the avocado halves or in a bowl as pictured.

Serve with the salad leaves and a sprinkling of paprika, salt and pepper.

SALAD DRESSING ESSENTIAL INGREDIENTS*

THESE ARE ALL THE INGREDIENTS I USE TO MAKE VARIOUS DRESSINGS TO KEEP THE PROTEIN SALADS NICE AND VARIED AND INTERESTING. YOU NEED A BASE OF $^2/_3$ VINEGAR $^1/_3$ OIL – THEN YOU CAN ADD IN CONDIMENTS ON TOP – I KNOW THIS MAKES MORE THAN ONE!

SOME CLASSICS ARE;

> HONEY AND MUSTARD – OLIVE OIL, MUSTARD, HONEY AND CIDER VINEGAR

> FRENCH – LEMON JUICE, OLIVE OIL, SALT AND PEPPER

> THAI – SESAME OIL, TAMARI SAUCE AND BALSAMIC VINEGAR

> HONEY AND WALNUT – RED WINE VINEGAR, HONEY, MUSTARD AND WALNUT OIL

> SATAY STYLE – PEANUT BUTTER, RAW GARLIC, HONEY, MUSTARD, WHITE WINE VINEGAR AND OLIVE OIL

ONCE YOU'VE GOT THE HANG OF THESE IMAGINATION IS THE LIMIT – YOU CAN KEEP THEM REALLY ZINGY WITH LOTS OF VINEGAR AND RAW GARLIC OR MELLOW THEM DOWN WITH MORE OIL AND LIGHTER CONDIMENTS IF YOU WISH.

VINEGAR

VINEGAR BEFORE A MEAL OR DURING LOWERS THE GLYCEMIC INDEX AND HELPS FAT MANAGEMENT AND BLOOD GLUCOSE CONTROL – A CAPFUL IN THE MORNINGS WITH WATER HELPS ALKALISE THE SYSTEM.

<LUNCH>

CAESAR SALAD *

<SERVES: 02>

<NUTRITION:>

PER SERVING:

> 250 KCAL

> 30G PROTEIN

> 14G CARBOHYDRATE

> 8G FAT

> *A CLASSIC SALAD AND ALL-TIME FAVOURITE. THE SECRET WHICH MAKES THIS HEALTHIER IS THE HOME-MADE CAESAR DRESSING.*

<INGREDIENTS:>

> 300G GRILLED CHICKEN, MARINATED IN GARLIC AND LEMON

> 1 HEAD ROMAINE LETTUCE

> 2 SLICES RYE BREAD, TOASTED AND CUT INTO SMALL PIECES

> 1 SMALL HANDFUL ALMONDS

> 3 EGG YOLKS, BEATEN

> 3 TBSP DIJON MUSTARD

> 8 GARLIC CLOVES

> 2 ANCHOVY FILLETS

> 6 CAPERS

> 1½ TSP SALT

> ½ TSP WHITE PEPPER

> ½ TSP DRIED OREGANO LEAVES

> 15 DROPS TABASCO SAUCE

> 15 DROPS WORCESTERSHIRE SAUCE

> OLIVE OIL, AS NEEDED

> 5 TSP WHITE WINE VINEGAR

<METHOD:>

Mix together the chicken, lettuce, rye bread pieces and the almonds and keep to one side.

Combine all remaining ingredients except the olive oil and vinegar in a blender on a low speed. Slowly add the olive oil until the mixture thickens to the consistency of mayonnaise, add the vinegar and blend.

Toss through with the mixed salad ingredients.

<LUNCH>

HAM BEETROOT TOMATO CARROT AND SAUERKRAUT SALAD*

<SERVES: 01>

 COLD CUTS AND SIMPLE SALAD INGREDIENTS CAN MAKE A QUICK SNACK OR STARTER TO A BIGGER MEAL. THE ORGANIC BEETROOT HAS A NUMBER OF HEALTH BENEFITS – ASSISTING CIRCULATION AND BLOOD PRESSURE TO NAME A COUPLE AND THE HAM TASTES GREAT.

<NUTRITION:>

PER SERVING:

> 495 KCAL

> 53G PROTEIN

> 26G CARBOHYDRATE

> 20G FAT

<INGREDIENTS:>

> 200G HAM

> 2 BEETROOT, COOKED

> 1 MEDIUM CARROT, GRATED

> 10 CHERRY TOMATOES

> 2 TBSP SAUERKRAUT

> 1 DSP CIDER VINEGAR

> 1 DSP OLIVE OIL

> 1 DSP DIJON MUSTARD

<METHOD:>

Lay all the ingredients out as desired.

Mix the cider vinegar, oilive oil and Dijon mustard together and pour over the salad and serve.

SHREDDED SPROUTING THAI SALAD*

<SERVES: 02>

<NUTRITION:>

PER SERVING:

> 240 KCAL

> 8G PROTEIN

> 20G CARBOHYDRATE

> 12G FAT

ORIENTAL SALADS LIKE THIS ARE ONE OF MY FAVOURITES. THE SWEET AND SALTY DRESSING WITH FISH SAUCE, CHEWY, SUCCULENT PRAWNS AND THE ROASTED NUTS ADD TEXTURES AND TASTES WHICH KEEP YOUR TASTEBUDS GUESSING. THE SPINS ON A BASIC PROTEIN SALAD ARE ENDLESS AND DELICIOUS PROOF THAT HEALTHY EATING DOES NOT HAVE TO BE BLAND AND BORING.

<INGREDIENTS:>

> 60G FENNEL BULB, GRATED

> 30G WHITE SAVOY CABBAGE HEART, SHREDDED

> 60G BEANSPROUTS

> 1 LARGE HANDFUL ALFALFA SPROUTS

> ¼ RED CABBAGE, FINELY CHOPPED

> 1 CARROT, CHOPPED OR FINELY SLICED

> 1 SMALL RED ONION, CHOPPED

> JUICE OF 1 LIME

> 1 DSP CHILLI SAUCE

> 1 TBSP FISH SAUCE

> 1 TSP PEANUT BUTTER

> 2 TBSP BALSAMIC VINEGAR

> 1 DSP SESAME OIL

<METHOD:>

Chop all the vegetables to your taste and mix together in a bowl.

In a jar with a lid on shake together all the remaining dressing ingredients, pour over the salad and serve.

ALTERNATIVES:

Replace vegetables with grated red cabbage, carrot and beetroot. Include a handful of prawns for an interesting twist and to up the protein component.

<INGREDIENTS>

EASTERN SPICES*

THE HEALTH BENEFITS OF THAI AND ORIENTAL CUISINE

Tom Yum soup is a great example of a food that is currently under scientific study for its health and immune enhancing benefits. Many of the other spices used in these type of cooking are also known for their immune enhancing, blood thinning and heart and cancer protective effects.

STARTING THESE DISHES WITH FRESH HERBS AND SPICES IS THE WAY TO GO. IF YOU CANNOT FIND THAI GINGER YOU CAN USE PLAIN GINGER, SHALLOTS AND ONIONS.

ADDED TO THESE MAY BE ANY OF THE FOLLOWING HERBS/SPICES:

> TURMERIC

> CORIANDER SEED

> LEMONGRASS

> FRESH OR DRIED CHILLIES

You can also use the Thai and Chinese pastes which are made from fresh spices and can be very tasty indeed. Mixing a few fresh herbs with the pastes brings an authentic feel back to the dish without you needing to go shopping for fresh spices and herbs all the time.

GARNISHES WITH FRESH HERBS FINISHES THESE DISHES OFF NICELY AS IT WILL DO WITH MOST OTHER DISHES – FRESH CORIANDER IS A PARTICULAR FAVOURITE OF MINE.

> FRESH CORIANDER LEAVES

> FRESH BASIL LEAVES

> SPRING ONION

> TURMERIC OR CURCUMIN

Curcumin is one of the most studied spices currently possessing massive anti inflammatory properties. It helps with all inflammatory conditions, from arthritis to cancer and heart disease. Muscle soreness and asthma. It keeps your blood thin and has an anti-bacterial and antioxidant effect.

TO ADD MORE TURMERIC TO YOUR DIET, TRY TO EAT CURRY (THE KIND THAT INCLUDES TURMERIC) AT LEAST ONCE A WEEK.

GALANGAL – THAI GINGER HAS MANY OF THE SAME BENEFITS OF STANDARD GINGER BUT SOME PEOPLE SAY IT'S MORE POWERFUL.

Both gingers **help with nausea, digestion, inflammation** including assisting arthritic pain. They also **contain anti-inflammatory components** like gingerols. Ginger also increases dopamine which makes it **good for get up and go in the mornings**.

CHILLIES (FRESH OR DRIED)

Recent human studies show that eating chillies **helps you sleep better, keeps your heart healthy through their blood thinning effect,** and **helps maintain consistent insulin and glucose levels.** They also help with fat burning and increase catchecholamines in the brain.

COCONUT MILK

For some reason coconut milk got a bad reputation the last century probably to do with large food conglomerates preferring palm oil. Coconut oil has excellent health benefits and **positive effects on blood cholesterol profiles**, it also **tastes great and has antifungal and bacterial effects** in the gut. Some people also swear by its **anti-ageing properties** – it seems to help with skin health for example.

LEMONGRASS

Lemongrass is used lots in all forms of Thai cooking – it has similar benefits to normal lemon zest and **has been used to treat a number of conditions such as flus and colds**, which may be why Tom Yum Soup is so good at relieving cold and flu symptoms.

> FEVERS

> HEADACHES

> ABDOMINAL PAIN AND OTHER STOMACH CONDITIONS

> ARTHRITIS

> FUNGAL CONDITIONS

CORIANDER

One thing to remember with coriander is that the seeds tend to contain more healing benefits than fresh leaves. It is particularly **good for stimulating appetites, the relief of gastrointestinal trouble (including gas and bloating), settling digestive problems** and **aiding bacterial and fungal infections.**

TOM YUM SOUP*

<SERVES: 01>

❝ BLOOD-THINNING SPICES AND HERBS ROUND OUT THIS POWERHOUSE OF A SOUP NICELY. GREAT EATEN ALONE AS A SNACK, SMALL MEAL OR TO START A MAIN MEAL. SOUPS TEND TO TAKE THE EDGE OFF YOUR APPETITE SO ARE USEFUL FOR PEOPLE WHO TEND TO OVEREAT.

<NUTRITION:>

PER SERVING:

> 175 KCAL

> 24G PROTEIN

> 9G CARBOHYDRATE

> 5G FAT

<INGREDIENTS:>

> 1 GARLIC CLOVE, CHOPPED

> 2 FRESH CHILLIS, CHOPPED

> 1 SMALL HANDFUL FRESH GINGER (OR THAI GINGER)

> 1 TBSP TOM YUM PASTE

> 600ML CHICKEN STOCK

> 1 SPRIG FRESH LEMONGRASS

> SALT AND PEPPER

> ½ X 400G CAN COCONUT MILK

> 200G KING PRAWNS

> CORIANDER (OR FLAT-LEAF PARSLEY), TO SERVE

<METHOD:>

Cook the garlic, chilli, ginger and Tom Yum paste in a pan over a medium heat.

Add everything but the prawns and garnishes and boil on a medium heat for 2 minutes.

Add the prawns, remove from the heat and leave until the prawns are opaque – around 2-3 minutes.

Serve with the chilli sprinkled over the top.

<LUNCH>

HAM AND WATERCRESS SOUP*

<SERVES: 01-02>

<NUTRITION:>

PER SERVING:

> 195 KCAL

> 32G PROTEIN

> 5G CARBOHYDRATE

> 5G FAT

A WINTER WARMER AND EXCELLENTLY NUTRITIONAL SPIN ON A PEA AND HAM SOUP. WATERCRESS HAS EXCEPTIONAL HEALING ABILITY FOR THE MUCOUS MEMBRANE.

<INGREDIENTS:>

> 200G FRESH WATERCRESS, RINSED AND DRAINED

> 1½ LITRES CHICKEN STOCK

> 150G HAM, CHOPPED

> 1 ONION, CHOPPED

> 2 BAY LEAVES

> SALT AND FRESHLY GROUND PEPPER, TO TASTE

<METHOD:>

Add the watercress and stock to a large pan, bring to the boil and skim off anything that forms on top.

Add the chopped onion and bay leaves and cook down until the mixture has reduced as desired– this usually takes around 20 minutes.

Remove from the heat and cool, then blend the soup into a smooth liquid. Return the mixture to the heat and add the ham ensure that it is warm throughout.

Season and serve.

CELERIAC AND JERUSALEM ARTICHOKE SOUP*

<SERVES: 04>

<NUTRITION:>

PER SERVING:

> 285 KCAL

> 12G PROTEIN

> 46G CARBOHYDRATE

> 6G FAT

❝ ARTICHOKE HAS TRADITIONALLY BEEN USED FOR LIVER SUPPORT AND CLEANSING OVER THE YEARS, AND IT'S GOT SOME GOOD RESEARCH TO SUPPORT THIS USE. CELERIAC IS GOOD SOURCE OF FIBRE, INCLUDING THE SOLUBLE TYPE THAT CAN LOWER ELEVATED BLOOD CHOLESTEROL. IT'S A GOOD SOURCE OF TRACE MINERALS AND IS LOW IN CARBS FOR A ROOT VEGGY – CELERIAC MASH IS AN EXCELLENT ALTERNATIVE TO HIGHER CARB MASH FROM OTHER POTATOES. SO THIS SOUP COMBINES EXCELLENT CLEANSING PROPERTIES WITH A HIGH NUTRIENT AND LOW CARB IMPACT. IF YOU ADDED SOME LEAN HAM OR OTHER PROTEIN SOURCE THROUGH THE MIXTURE YOU'D BRING IT UP TO A COMPLETE MEAL AND NOT JUST A SNACK OR STARTER.

<INGREDIENTS:>

> BUTTER, FOR FRYING

> 100G CELERIAC, PEELED AND DICED

> 100G JERUSALEM ARTICHOKES, SCRUBBED AND DICED

> 1 LITRE GOOD CHICKEN STOCK

> SALT AND PEPPER, TO TASTE

> ½ TSP GROUND NUTMEG

> 4 TBSP CREME FRAICHE (OR SOUR CREAM), TO SERVE

<METHOD:>

Melt the butter in a pan then add the prepared celeriac and Jerusalem artichokes and sweat until they begin to soften.

Add the stock and simmer for 15-20 minutes until the vegetables are tender. Blend and season to taste with the salt, pepper and nutmeg.

Add the crème fraîche, 1 tablespoon per bowl, and serve.

SALMON AND SPINACH QUICHE*

<NUTRITION:>

PER SERVING:

> 540 KCAL

> 24G PROTEIN

> 22G CARBOHYDRATE

> 40G FAT

<SERVES: 06>

> THE BEAUTY OF A FLAN OR QUICHE IS YOU CAN MAKE THEM FROM ALMOST ANY LEFTOVERS AND THEY MAKE OTHER PROTEINS GO A REALLY LONG WAY. THE GAMMON ROAST CAN BE CONVERTED EASILY ENOUGH INTO A HAM AND CHEESE QUICHE AND IT CAN BE EATEN WITH ANYTHING ELSE OR AS A STANDALONE SNACK. IT'S A HIGH PROTEIN TO CARBOHYDRATE RATIO TOO.

<INGREDIENTS:>

> 170G FLOUR

> 1 EGG YOLK

> 85G BUTTER

> 2 TBSP COLD WATER

> 2 SMALL RED ONIONS, FINELY DICED

> 1 TBSP OLIVE OIL

> 2 SALMON FILLETS, COOKED AND FLAKED

> 4 CUBES SPINACH, COOKED

> 2 EGGS

> 5 TBSP GOAT'S MILK

> 5 TBSP HALF-FAT CREME FRAICHE

> 150G GRATED CHEESE

> 57G BUTTER

> SALT AND PEPPER, TO TASTE

<METHOD:>

Preheat the oven to 150ºC.

Mix together the flour, egg yolk, butter and water in a food blender until it forms a smooth dough. Bake blind in a 25cm flan dish with baking beans for 15 minutes – this seals the pastry so the sauce doesn't go soggy in the quiche.

Soften the onions in the oil and add the salmon. Add to the pastry case with the spinach – ensuring they are evenly spaced in the dish.

Mix together the eggs, milk, crème fraîche, cheese and butter and pour this mixture over the onion, salmon and spinach in the case. Season with salt and pepper.

Cook in the oven for 40 minutes.

<DINNER>

MEALS ARE A GREAT TIME FOR SHARING AND THIS WIDE SELECTION OF HOT AND COLD DISHES

ARE HEALTHY, HIGH PROTEIN VERSIONS OF CLASSICS — MAKING IT EASY TO PLEASE EVERYONE

<DINNER>

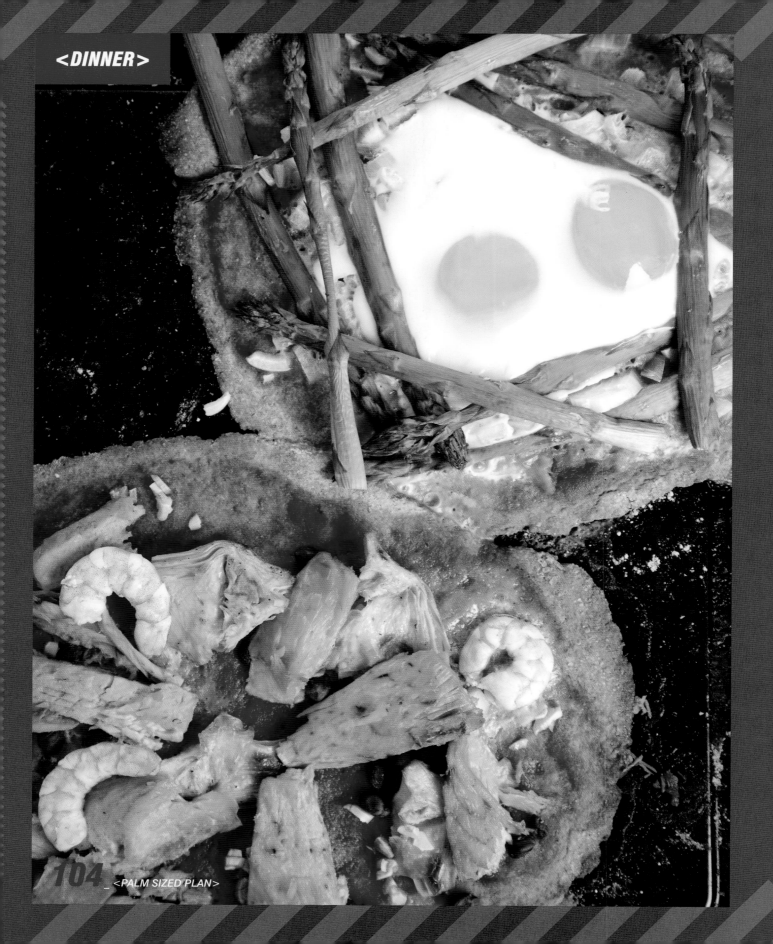

> WE ALL GET THE ODD NIGHT WHEN WE'RE TEMPTED TO CALL IN A CURRY OR CHINESE – FORTIFIED PIZZA IS ONE QUICK AND EASY WAY TO AVOID THIS TEMPTATION, ENJOY SOMETHING FAST AND SATISFYING AND YOU'LL SAVE A BIT OF CASH. YOU CAN MAKE YOUR OWN BASE OR USE A PRE-MADE ONE AND ADD YOUR OWN INGREDIENTS.

WHOLEMEAL PIZZA BASE*
<SERVES: 02>

<INGREDIENTS:>

> 250G STRONG WHOLEMEAL BREAD FLOUR (OR '00' FLOUR)

> ½ TSP FINE SEA SALT

> ½ X 7G SACHET DRIED YEAST

> ½ TSP GOLDEN CASTER SUGAR

> 1 TBSP EXTRA VIRGIN OLIVE OIL

> 175ML LUKEWARM WATER

<METHOD:>

Sieve the flour and salt on to a clean work surface and make a well in the middle.

Mix together the yeast, sugar and olive oil into the water and leave for a few minutes, then pour into the well. Using a fork, bring the flour in gradually from the sides and swirl it into the liquid.

Keep mixing, drawing larger amounts of flour in, and when it all starts to come together, work the rest of the flour in with clean, flour-dusted hands – knead well.

Place the ball of dough in a large flour-dusted bowl and lightly flour the top of the dough. Cover the bowl with a damp cloth and place in a warm room for about an hour until the dough has doubled in size.

When the dough has doubled, remove and place on a flour-dusted surface. Knead by pushing the air out with your hands. Either use immediately or wrap in cling film and store in the fridge (or freezer) until required.

NEPTUNO PIZZA*
<SERVES: 02>

<NUTRITION:>
PER SERVING:

> 680 KCAL

> 66G PROTEIN

> 70G CARBOHYDRATE

> 15G FAT

<INGREDIENTS:>

> WHOLEMEAL PIZZA DOUGH (SEE RECIPE ON LEFT)

> PASSATA, TO COVER BASE

> 1 CLOVE OF GARLIC, CHOPPED

> 1 SMALL CAN PRESERVED ARTICHOKES HEARTS

> 1 CAN ALBACORE TUNA

> 250G KING PRAWNS, COOKED

> 1 HANDFUL CAPERS

<METHOD:>

Split the dough to make two balls, roll each ball out in order to make a round pizza base. Place on a lightly greased tray and spread passata to the edge of the dough. Spread the remaining ingredients evenly over the passata and cook for 20-25 minutes at 170ºC.

VEGETARIAN EGG AND ASPARAGUS PIZZA*
<SERVES: 02>

<NUTRITION:>
PER SERVING:

> 505 KCAL

> 30G PROTEIN

> 65G CARBOHYDRATE

> 14G FAT

<INGREDIENTS:>

> WHOLEMEAL PIZZA DOUGH (SEE RECIPE ON LEFT)

> PASSATA, TO COVER BASE

> 1 GARLIC CLOVE, CHOPPED

> 1 SMALL ONION, CHOPPED

> 2 EGGS

> 6-7 ASPARAGUS SPEARS

<METHOD:>

Split the dough to make two balls, roll each ball out in order to make a round pizza base. Place on a lightly greased tray and spread passata to the edge of the dough.

Spread the remaining ingredients accept the eggs evenly over the passata.

Just before cooking, crack both the eggs over the pizza (they will fry as the pizza cooks) and cook for 20-25 minutes at 170ºC.

< DINNER >

BEEF FILLET ASPARAGUS SALSA VERDE AND PORTUGUESE POTATOES*

<SERVES: 01>

<NUTRITION:>

PER SERVING:

> 735 KCAL

> 70G PROTEIN

> 45G CARBOHYDRATE

> 32G FAT

" SIMPLE STEAK AND VEGGIES ALWAYS NEEDS A GOOD STRONG CONDIMENT TO CUT THROUGH THE POWERFUL FLAVOURS AND BRING THE ASPARAGUS TO LIFE. STEAK FILLET IS THE LEANEST CUT AND ASPARAGUS IS ONE OF THE LOWEST CARB HIGH FIBRE VEGETABLES – USED IN ORIENTAL MEDICINE TO CLEANSE THE LIVER.

<INGREDIENTS:>

> 20ML COCONUT OIL

> 1KG POTATOES

> 2 RED ONIONS, CHOPPED

> 1 HANDFUL WHOLE BLACK PEPPERCORNS

> 1 GARLIC BULB, CRUSHED

> 1 LARGE FILLET STEAK

> 6 ASPARAGUS SPEARS

> 5 ANCHOVY FILLETS

> 5 GARLIC CLOVES

> 1 PINCH OF SALT

> 3 TBSP RED WINE VINEGAR

> 1 TBSP DIJON MUSTARD

> 1 HANDFUL CAPERS

> 1 BUNCH FRESH PARSLEY

> 1 LARGE HANDFUL FRESH MINT

<METHOD:>

To make the Portuguese potatoes heat the coconut oil in a tray in a warm oven around 180ºC. Cut the potatoes in half and coat in the hot oil, draining any excess oil from the pan before returning to the oven.

Add the onions, peppercorns and garlic to the pan and roast at 180ºC for 40 minutes up to 1 hour.

Pan-fry the steak according to how you like it – this one was done over a medium heat for 8 minutes each side for medium rare.

For the salsa verde put all the remaining ingredients in a blender and blitz until smooth.

To serve steam the asparagus for 5 minutes and serve with Portugese potatoes, asparagus and salsa verde.

"THE POTATOES AND SALSA VERDE MAKE GREAT ACCOMPANIMENTS FOR OTHER DISHES TOO."
<MATT LOVELL>

<DINNER>

BOLOGNESE*

<SERVES: 02>

" LEAN STEAK MINCE BOLOGNESE WITH A BASE OF ONION, GARLIC, CELERY AND CARROT, LOADED WITH FRESH OR TINNED TOMATOES, HERBS, STOCK, SPICES – IS BURSTING WITH GOODNESS AND FLAVOUR. IF YOU'VE HAD A MONSTER WORKOUT THEN YOU CAN CHOW DOWN ON SOME SPAGHETTI OR PASTA – FOR EVERYONE ELSE WHO'S SEEKING TO STAY TRIM AND DROP A FEW POUNDS THEN LEEK LINGUINE IS THE WAY TO GO. YOU CAN ALSO MAKE LEEK SPAGHETTI BY SLICING IT THINLY LONG WAYS – FOR THE LINGUINE YOU DO THE SAME BUT IN THICK STRIPS AND MELT IT DOWN IN A PAN ON A LOW HEAT UNTIL IT CARAMELISES A LITTLE.

<INGREDIENTS:>

> 5 GARLIC CLOVES, FINELY CHOPPED

> 1 ONION

> 2 LARGE CARROTS, FINELY CHOPPED

> 3 CELERY STICKS, FINELY CHOPPED

> 1 TSP COCONUT OIL

> 300G LEAN MINCED BEEF

> 1 PINCH FRESH OREGANO

> 1 PINCH PAPRIKA

> 1 PINCH SALT

> 1 PINCH PEPPER

> 100G CHICKEN LIVERS

> 1 SMALL GLASS RED WINE

> 2 DSP TOMATO PUREE

> 350ML PASSATTA

> 1 PINT CHICKEN STOCK

> 1 LEEK

<METHOD:>

Soften the garlic, onion, carrots and celery in the coconut oil in a pan over a medium heat.

In a separate pan cook the meat including chicken livers over a medium heat until brown then add the oregano and paprika, salt and pepper. Drain the fat from the meat and add the vegetables to the mix.

Add the liquid ingredients and simmer and reduce until a thick consistency is achieved.

For the leek linguine, slice one leek thinly long ways in to ½ cm strips. Transfer the sliced leek to a frying pan adding a little water, just enough to stop the leeks from sticking. Cover the leeks with a lid and melt them in a pan on a low heat until they caramelise a little, check these every 5 minutes and remove when golden.

ALTERNATIVE:

The bolognese can be served with broccoli (200g per serving) or spaghetti (75g per serving).

<DINNER>

CHILLI*

<SERVES: 01>

> **THE BOLOGNESE SAUCE CAN BE EASILY CONVERTED INTO A CHILLI WITH THE ADDITION OF ONE OR TWO INGREDIENTS. I LIKE TO ADD SOME DARK CHOCOLATE AND KIDNEY BEANS WITH THEIR UNIQUE BLOOD GLUCOSE STABILISING EFFECT AND POTENTIAL BODY COMPOSITION BENEFITS TOO. A PERFECT METHOD OF REVAMPING LEFTOVERS, YOU CAN TRANSFER HALF THE BOLOGNESE INTO A CHILLI TO KEEP THINGS FRESH.**

<INGREDIENTS:>

> ½ BOLOGNESE RECIPE (SEE PAGE 108)

> ½ TSP GROUND CORIANDER

> ½ TSP GROUND GINGER

> ½ TSP CHILLI FLAKES

> 1 DSP COCOA POWDER OR 4 SQUARES DARK CHOCOLATE

> 120G KIDNEY BEANS, DRAINED

> 1 TBSP CREME FRAICHE

> 75G WHOLEGRAIN RICE

<METHOD:>

Dry fry toast the ground coriander, ginger and the chilli flakes on a low heat until they are slightly brown.

Heat the bolognese and stir in the seasonings, cocoa powder or dark chocolate and kidney beans.

Cook the rice as desired.

Serve the chilli either on its own with a tablespoon of crème fraîche or on a bed of wholegrain rice.

LASAGNE*

<SERVES: 04>

<NUTRITION:>

PER SERVING:

> 480 KCAL

> 30G PROTEIN

> 50G CARBOHYDRATE

> 18G FAT

❝❝ *A HIGH MEAT SAUCE TO PASTA RATIO MAKES THIS A GREAT RECOVERY OR FUELLING MIX, ALTERNATIVELY SPINACH PASTA AND RICOTTA CAN BE USED TO ALTER THE DISH IF YOU FANCY, ALTHOUGH HIGH QUALITY MINCE IS A MUST.*

<INGREDIENTS:>

> 1 TSP OLIVE OIL

> 1 LARGE ONION, CHOPPED

> 2 GARLIC CLOVES, CHOPPED

> 2 CELERY STICKS, CHOPPED

> 2 CARROTS, CHOPPED

> 500G LEAN MINCED BEEF

> 100G CHICKEN LIVERS, CHOPPED

> SALT AND PEPPER, TO TASTE

> 1 SMALL GLASS RED WINE

> 1 DSP TARRAGON, CHOPPED

> 2 BAY LEAVES

> 1 X 440G CAN TOMATOES, CHOPPED
  (OR 200ML PASSATA)

> 1 DSP TOMATO PUREE

> 2 TBSP SPELT FLOUR

> 2 DSP OLIVE OIL

> 450ML SKIMMED MILK

> 6 LASAGNE SHEETS

> 1 WHOLE REDUCED FAT MOZZARELLA,
  SLICED INTO ROUNDS

> PARMESAN (OR CHEDDAR), GRATED

<METHOD:>

Preheat the oven to 180°C.

Brown the onion, garlic, celery and carrots in the olive oil until the onion is translucent, then add the meat and livers util cooked through. Season, add the wine and reduce a little before adding the herbs, tomatoes/passata and tomato purée. Simmer for 20-25 minutes.

Meanwhile make the béchamel sauce by combining the flour and 2 dessert spoons of olive oil into a paste over the heat. Cook through and add the milk gradually while whisking to thicken.

Assemble the lasagne by alternating the meat with the lasagne sheets and béchamel sauce, finally topping with the slices of mozzarella and sprinkle with the parmesan/cheddar.

Bake in the oven for 35 minutes.

ALTERNATIVE:

For a lower fat lasagne substitute the beef mince with turkey mince – this gives stats of KCAL 400, FAT 10g per portion.

<QUICK TIP>

HOW TO SEASON A CHICKEN*

<1> GET A SMALL SHARP KNIFE AND PUSH THIS INTO THE FLESH OF THE BREAST TO MAKE SMALL OPENINGS.

<2> PUSH HERBS SUCH AS ROSEMARY FIRMLY INTO THE INCISION.

<3> THEN PUSH CHOPPED GARLIC INTO THE INCISION.

<4> DO THIS ALL OVER THE CHICKEN FOCUSING ON THE LEGS AND BREAST.

1.

2.

3.

4.

<PALM SIZED PLAN>_

<DINNER>

ROAST CHICKEN AND VEGETABLES*

<SERVES: 04>

❝ THE ROAST IS A VERSATILE AND DELICIOUSLY NUTRITIOUS CHOICE FOR THE WEEKEND. THE BONES OF COURSE CAN BE USED TO MAKE A RECOVERY STOCK. THE COMPONENTS – MEAT, VEGGIES AND STARCH – MAKE A MIXED MEAL AND YOU CAN GO TO TOWN ON THE TRIMMINGS IF YOU WISH TO.

<INGREDIENTS:>

> 1 MEDIUM ORGANIC CHICKEN, ENOUGH TO FEED 4 PEOPLE

> 1 LARGE HANDFUL ROSEMARY SPRIGS

> 6 GARLIC CLOVES, SLICED INTO SMALL LENGTHS

> 20ML COCONUT OIL

> 3 RAW BEETROOTS, ROUGHLY CHOPPED AND SCRUBBED

> 3 LARGE CARROTS, QUARTERED

<METHOD:>

Preheat the oven to 180ºC.

Prick the chicken skin then make slits in the flesh with a knife, add the rosemary and slip some garlic alongside. Do this all over the breasts and legs.

Cover your hands with coconut oil and rub the beetroot and carrots until lightly coated.

Add the vegetables around the outside of the chicken. Roast in the oven for 1 hour, then turn the chicken onto the breast side and continue cooking for another 30-45 minutes or until skin is golden and the juices run clear.

Serve with the vegetables.

<DINNER>

SWEET AND SOUR CHICKEN*

<SERVES: 02>

THIS IS AN EASY WAY TO TOP UP GLYCOGEN RESERVES AHEAD OF A BIG ENDURANCE EVENT OR TO RECOVERY FROM A HARD DAY'S ACTIVITY.

<NUTRITION:>

PER SERVING:

> 260 KCAL

> 30G PROTEIN

> 30G CARBOHYDRATE

> 2.5G FAT

<INGREDIENTS:>

> 1 ORGANIC CHICKEN BREAST, CHOPPED

> 3 GARLIC CLOVES

> 2 HEAPED TSP CHINESE FIVE SPICE

> 1 DSP SESAME SEED OIL

> 3 CELERY STICKS

> 2 CARROTS

> 1 SMALL RED ONION

> 1 X 227G CAN PINEAPPLE CHUNKS, IN JUICE

> 50ML HOME-MADE KETCHUP

> 1 X 225G CAN BAMBOO SHOOTS

> 1 HANDFUL BABY SWEETCORN

> 1 HANDFUL MANGE TOUT

> JUICE OF ½ A LEMON

> 50G BASMATI RICE

<METHOD:>

Fry the chicken, garlic and spices in the sesame oil, when browned, add the celery, carrots and onion.

Cook until warmed through, add all the other ingredients and cover the pan.

Continue cooking for another 15 minutes or until the chicken is fully cooked.

Serve on a bed of basmati rice.

<DINNER>

CORONATION CHICKEN*

<SERVES: 06>

<NUTRITION:>

PER SERVING:

> 480 KCAL

> 40G PROTEIN

> 30G CARBOHYDRATE

> 22G FAT

" THE ENGLISH CLASSIC – AND A PERSONAL FAVOURITE OF MINE. THIS MAKES A PERFECT HIGH PROTEIN AND HIGH-CARB RECOVERY MEAL. IT'S A PERFECT COMBINATION OF SPICES, SAUCE AND INGREDIENTS FROM AROUND THE GLOBE.

<INGREDIENTS:>

> 600G CHICKEN BREAST PIECES

> 1 BAY LEAF

> 15 PEPPERCORNS

> 1 STALK CELERY

> 1 SMALL ONION

> 1 TBSP OLIVE OIL

> 2 TSP CURRY POWDER

> 1 TBSP RED WINE

> LEMON JUICE, TO TASTE

> 1 TSP TOMATO PUREE

> 2 TSP NO ADDED SUGAR APRICOT JAM

> 90G LOW-FAT MAYONNAISE

> 300G WILD AND BASMATI RICE

> 300G PEAS

> ALMOND FLAKES, AS NEEDED

<METHOD:>

Poach the chicken for 1 hour 15 minutes in filtered water with the bay leaf, peppercorns and celery.

While this is poaching fry the onion in the olive oil until soft, then add the curry powder and stir through. Add the wine, lemon juice, apricot jam and tomato purée and continue stirring. Set the sauce aside and leave to cool.

Once the chicken is cooked allow the water to cool – this will allow the chicken to absorb some of the water and moisten it up a bit. Shred the chicken.

Stir the mayonnaise into the curry sauce and add the shredded chicken.

Boil the rice and follow the instructions for cooking, 3 minutes before the rice has finished cooking, strain and add the peas to the mixture.

Serve the rice and peas on a plate in the shape of a ring and add the chicken mixed with the sauce in the middle. Adding almond flakes finishes the dish off nicely.

"THIS IS ACTUALLY A VERY LOW-FAT DISH IF YOU USE LOW-FAT MAYONNAISE – THE BEAUTY IS IN THE ABILITY YOU HAVE TO TWEAK THE INGREDIENTS, ADDING MORE CURRY, GARLIC AND ALSO APRICOT JAM"
<MATT LOVELL>

<DINNER>

POT-ROASTED GUINEA FOWL IN GINGER WINE*

<SERVES: 02>

<NUTRITION:>

PER SERVING:

> 390 KCAL

> 57G PROTEIN

> 20G CARBOHYDRATE

> 9G FAT

" POT ROASTS OR HOT ROASTS ARE A GREAT WINTER DISH WHICH TAKE LITTLE TIME TO PREPARE AND CAN BE COOKED ON A SLOW COOKER FOR SAFETY (IF YOU GO OUT) OR LEFT IN THE OVEN WHILE YOU DO SOME OTHER JOBS. GAME SUCH AS GUINEA FOWL IS GREAT EATEN AS A REGULAR PART OF YOUR QUALITY PROTEIN INTAKE.

<INGREDIENTS:>

> 1 GUINEA FOWL

> 2 CARROTS, CHOPPED

> 3 CELERY STALKS, CHOPPED

> 1 RED ONION, CHOPPED

> SALT AND PEPPER, TO TASTE

> COCONUT OIL, AS NEEDED

> 125ML BRANDY

> 125ML GINGER WINE

> 2 DSP STEM GINGER

> 1 CINNAMON STICK

> 125ML ORANGE JUICE

> 200ML STRONG GAME STOCK

<METHOD:>

Season the bird all over and brown in the coconut oil over a medium heat.

Fry the onions, carrots, celery in a pan on a lower heat so they don't burn for 5-10 minutes or until these are softened slightly.

Add the brandy and flambé then add the remaining ingredients.

Continue cooking in the oven or a slow cooker.

For oven cooking cook for 3-4 hours at 150°C or for 2 hours at 180°C, to cook in a slow cooker follow the manufacturer's instructions.

<DINNER>

TURKEY FAJITAS*

<SERVES: 02>

<NUTRITION:>

PER SERVING:

> 290 KCAL

> 30G PROTEIN

> 35G CARBOHYDRATE

> 15G FAT

> *A NATIONAL FAVOURITE – EASY TO PREPARE AND EAT. LOW IN CARBOHYDRATES AS LONG AS YOU LOAD THE FILLING UP WELL AND OTHER MEXICAN CONDIMENTS CAN BE EASILY INTEGRATED SUCH AS SALSA OR GUACAMOLE.*

<INGREDIENTS:>

> 2 TURKEY BREASTS, CHOPPED

> OIL, FOR FRYING

> 1 TSP CUMIN SEEDS

> 1 TSP CHILLI

> 1 TSP PAPRIKA

> 4 GARLIC CLOVES, CHOPPED

> 2 ONIONS, CHOPPED

> 1 TSP ONION POWDER

> 1 DSP OREGANO

> 2 YELLOW PEPPERS, CHOPPED

> 2 CORN TORTILLAS

> SOUR CREAM (OR LOW-FAT CREME FRAICHE), AS DESIRED

> LEMON JUICE, TO TASTE

> CORIANDER LEAVES TO DECORATE BEFORE SERVING

<METHOD:>

Fry the turkey on a high heat in the oil with the cumin seeds, chilli, paprika and garlic for around 10-15 minutes until cooked.

Add the onions, onion powder, oregano and peppers until lightly cooked. Remove from the heat and sprinkle with the coriander leaves.

Heat the corn tortillas until soft in a pan or in the oven for 5 minutes at 180ºC.

Spoon the cooked meat and onions into the tortilla, and wrap up with a dollop of sour cream/crème fraîche and a squeeze of lemon juice.

<DINNER>

PORK AND PRUNES*

<SERVES: 03>

<NUTRITION:>

PER SERVING:

> 635 KCAL

> 45G PROTEIN

> 46G CARBOHYDRATE

> 31G FAT

 *THIS IS A CLASSIC DISH WHICH YOU CAN EAT WITH FRIENDS FOR A CLASSY DINNER PARTY OR WITH SOME SIMPLE TWEAKS IT MAKES A GREAT RECOVERY MEAL WHEN SERVED WITH RICE. PRUNES SCORE VERY HIGH ON THE ORAC SCALE, MEANING YOU GET LOTS OF PROTECTION FROM EATING THEM. THEY ALSO HELP KEEP YOU REGULAR! PORK LOIN OFFERS QUALITY LOW-FAT PROTEIN TO REBUILD ACHING MUSCLES.*

<INGREDIENTS:>

> 24 GIANT PRUNES

> ½ BOTTLE MEDIUM DRY WHITE WINE

> 500G PORK LOIN

> SEA SALT AND PEPPER, TO TASTE

> SPELT FLOUR, AS NEEDED

> 15G COCONUT OIL

> 1 TBSP REDCURRANT JELLY

> 250G GREEK YOGHURT

<METHOD:>

Place the soaked prunes in the oven at 160ºC for 2 minutes, making sure the liquid doesn't boil away.

Cut the pork loin into mini medallions, coat with flour, and season with salt and pepper. Fry the pork in the coconut oil until golden brown on both sides, set aside and leave the meat juices in the pan.

Drain the prune juice into the meat juices and add the prunes to the pork.

In a pan simmer the meat juices and prune juice, stirring in the redcurrant jelly.

Finally stir in the cream or Greek yoghurt, taking care not to curdle the sauce.

Pour over the pork while still hot and serve.

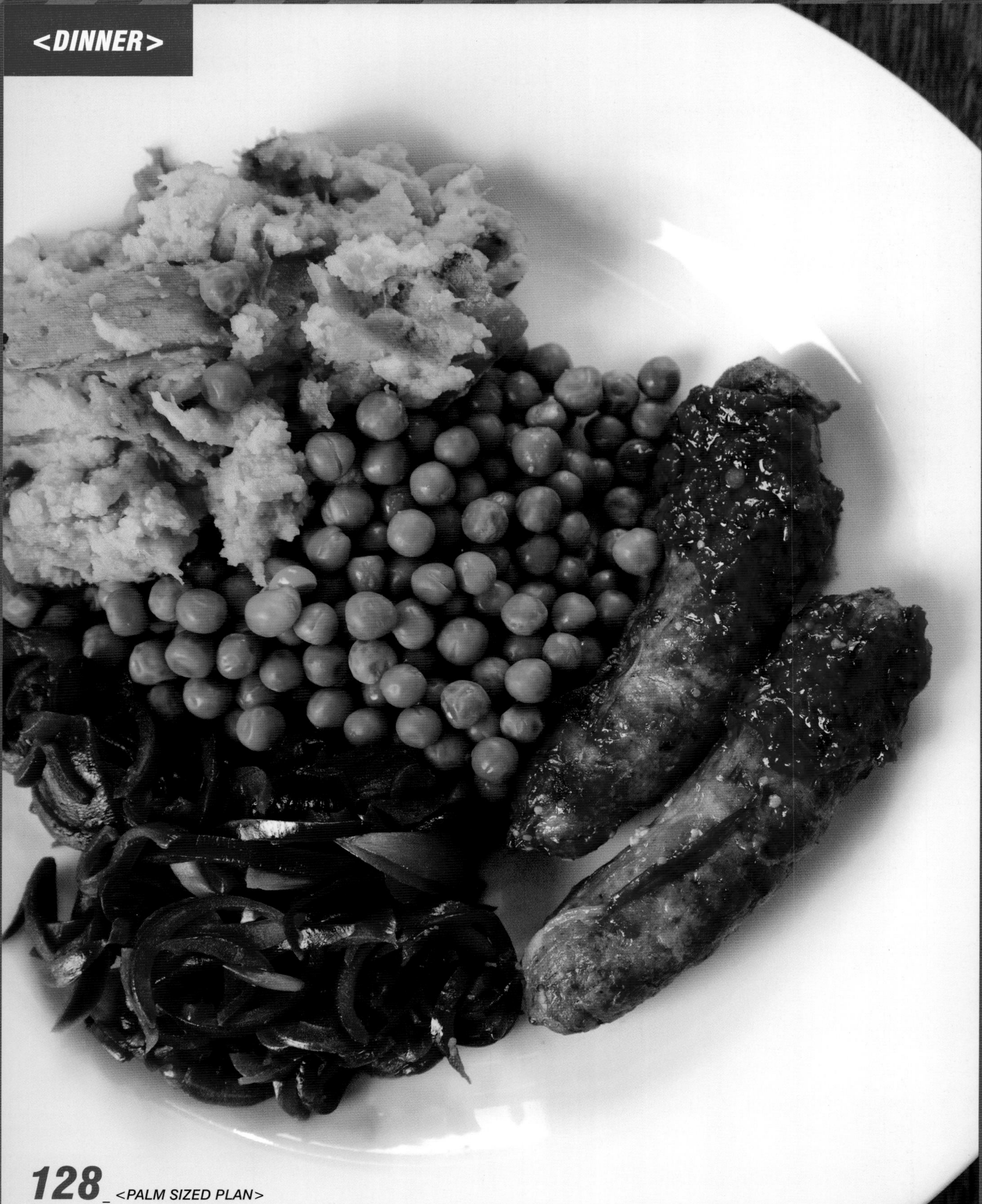

SAUSAGE AND MASH WITH RED ONIONS AND HARISSA PASTE*

<SERVES: 01>

 THE SECRET FOR THIS DISH IS IN THE INGREDIENTS –
A 97% MEAT SAUSAGE MAKES FOR A GOOD PROTEIN:FAT
CONTENT RATIO. THE SWEET POTATO MASH IS HIGH IN ENERGY
AND LOW ON THE GI SCALE, PLUS IT'S ONE OF THE HIGHEST
NUTRIENT DENSE STARCHY CARBOHYDRATES ALONG WITH
MAJESTY POTATOES AND BLACK WILD RICE.

<NUTRITION:>

PER SERVING:

> 875 KCAL

> 40G PROTEIN

> 95G CARBOHYDRATE

> 37G FAT

<INGREDIENTS:>

> 2 97% MEAT SAUSAGES

> 2 LARGE SWEET POTATOES, WITH SKINS

> 1 DSP COCONUT OIL

> 150G ORGANIC GARDEN PEAS

> 1 RED ONION, SLICED

> HOME-MADE KETCHUP, TO SERVE

> 1 DSP HARISSA PASTE

<METHOD:>

Prick then grill the sausages on a medium heat until brown throughout.

Meanwhile boil the potatoes for 10-15 minutes over a medium heat until soft and then mash together with the coconut oil.

Cook the peas as desired. Caramelise the onions in a pan until brown, gradually sweating them down on a low heat, taking care not to burn them. Cook for around 10 minutes keeping a lid on for the majority of cooking. Taking it off shortly before serving.

Plate up and serve with home-made ketchup.

"OTHER SAUSAGES YOU COULD USE ARE VENISON OR BEEF."
<MATT LOVELL>

<DINNER>

HEALTHY SHEPHERD'S PIE*

<SERVES: 04>

> **THE BOLOGNESE SAUCE IS SO VERSATILE – ALL YOU NEED TO DO IS CHANGE THE MEAT USED. THE ADVANTAGE OF MAKING THE MIX WITH THE LAMB IS YOU CAN CONVERT THIS STRAIGHT OVER TO THE MOROCCAN LAMB AND COUS COUS RECIPES WITH THE ADDITION OF A FEW EXTRA SPICES. MAKING MASS AMOUNTS OF BASE INGREDIENTS MEANS THEY CAN BE CONVERTED WITH SIMPLE TWEAKS TO REDUCE THE HASSLE FACTOR AROUND HEALTHY EATING AND PREPARATION.**

<INGREDIENTS:>

> 800G POTATOES

> 4 GARLIC CLOVES, CHOPPED

> 3 MEDIUM RED ONIONS, CHOPPED

> 2 LARGE CARROTS, CHOPPED

> 3 CELERY STICKS, CHOPPED

> COCONUT OIL, FOR FRYING

> 500G LEAN MINCED LAMB

> 1 DSP MIXED HERBS

> 1 SPRIG ROSEMARY

> SALT AND PEPPER, TO TASTE

> 400ML PASSATA

> 2 SMALL GLASSES RED WINE

> 200G PEAS

> 1 TBSP OLIVE OIL

> SKIMMED MILK, AS DESIRED

> 1 CHICKEN STOCK CUBE

<METHOD:>

Boil the potatoes still in their skins over a medium heat until cooked through, while they are cooking soften the garlic, onions, carrots and the celery in oil in a pan.

Add the meat until cooked through, then add the herbs, salt, pepper, passata and wine and simmer over a medium heat until the mix reaches a thick consistency. Add the peas and pour the mixture out into a bowl.

When the potatoes are cooked, mash them together with the olive oil and skimmed milk until they are soft.

Before spreading mix in the crushed stock cube. Cover the meat mixture with the mashed potato and oven bake at 180°C for 20 minutes until the potato topping is crispy.

ALTERNATIVE:

For Venison Cottage Pie, replace the minced lamb with lean minced venison together with a tablespoon of juniper berries added with the passata and wine.

Arrange as above and cook at a slightly lower heat of 160°C for 20 minutes or until the potato topping is crispy.

<DINNER>

KEBAB AND BEAN DAHL *

<SERVES: 02>

<NUTRITION:>

PER SERVING:

> 260 KCAL

> 20G PROTEIN

> 35G CARBOHYDRATE

> 5G FAT

THE KEBAB WHEN MADE PROPERLY REPRESENTS ALL THE MAJOR FOOD GROUPS AND CAN ACTUALLY BE INCREDIBLY HEALTHY – CHICKEN SHEESH FOR EXAMPLE, THE CHOICE OF THE DISCERNING REVELLER. I ALWAYS USED TO OPT FOR RED CABBAGE, CHILLI SAUCE AND GARLIC DRESSING TO UP THE PHYTONUTRIENT CONTENT OF THIS MIDNIGHT FEAST. BELOW IS A VERSION YOU CAN DO AT HOME WHICH IS ACE FOR LARGER BARBECUES.

<INGREDIENTS:>

> 250G MINCED LAMB

> 1 EGG

> 1 TSP EACH CUMIN, CORIANDER SEEDS, PAPRIKA, CHILLI, CINNAMON

> LEMON PEEL JUICE, TO MARINADE

> 1 ONION, FINELY CHOPPED

> 2 TSP EACH CORIANDER, CUMIN, PAPRIKA, GINGER, CINNAMON, GARAM MASALA

> ½ TSP CHILLI POWDER

> 2 TSP COCONUT OIL

> 1 GARLIC CLOVE

> 45G CHICKPEAS OR LENTILS, COOKED

> 45G BLACK-EYED PEAS

> 1 X 440G CAN CANNELLINI BEANS

> 2 TSP TOMATO PUREE

> SEASAME SEEDS, TO SERVE

<METHOD:>

Mash the mince, egg, single teaspoon of spices and lemon juice up with your hands making sure they are fully mixed. leave to rest for 30 minutes or overnight if possible.

For the dahl, soften the onion and spices together in the oil. Add the remaining ingredients and simmer until soft for around 20 minutes.

Mash some of the beans with a wooden spoon and set to one side

Returning to the kebabs make some small beef patties and gently fry over a medium heat for around 10 minutes until cooked.

Serve the dahl together with the kebabs a sprinkling of sesame seeds and chilli sauce.

<DINNER>

SPICY MOROCCAN LAMB COUS COUS*

<SERVES: 02>

 **YOU CAN USE THE SHEPHERD'S PIE BASE FOR THIS ULTIMATE MOROCCAN RESTORER. COUS COUS IS AN EASY DIGESTING SOURCE OF CARBOHYDRATES AND IF YOU DON'T LIKE WHEAT YOU CAN GET BELAZU BARLEY COUS COUS IN MOST SUPERMARKETS.**

<NUTRITION:>

PER SERVING:

> 400 KCAL

> 30G PROTEIN

> 50G CARBOHYDRATE

> 10G FAT

<INGREDIENTS:>

> 200G COUS COUS

> 1 X SHEPHERD'S PIE MINCE RECIPE (SEE PAGE 130)

> 1 RED CHILLI

> 1 RED PEPPER

> 1 TBSP MOROCCAN MIXED SPICE (OR 1/3 TBSP EACH CUMIN, PAPRIKA AND CINNAMON)

<METHOD:>

Place the cous cous in a pan, cover with boiling water,so that two-thirds is cous cous and a third water and cook over a medium heat for 5 minutes.

To the Shepherd's pie mince mix add a freshly chopped chilli, one red pepper and the Moroccan spice mix.

Cook the meat mix in a pan over a medium heat until the chilli softens.

When cooked stir in the cooked cous cous and serve. Harissa paste can be added if wished.

<DINNER>

CASSOULET*

<SERVES: 04>

FRENCH CLASSICS LIKE CASSOULET (CASSOULET) SHOULD BE ENJOYED WITH A GOOD GLASS OF RED WINE. ALCOHOL CONSUMPTION OF 8-10 UNITS ACTUALLY HAS A BETTER EFFECT ON HEALTH THAN NOT DRINKING AT ALL! BUT BEWARE THE POWER OF ALCOHOL AND IF THIS IS YOUR VICE READ THE CHAPTER ON ADDICTION TO HELP YOU CURB YOUR CRAVINGS.

<NUTRITION:>

PER SERVING:

> 330 KCAL

> 40G PROTEIN

> 12G CARBOHYDRATE

> 14G FAT

<INGREDIENTS:>

> 250G PORK BELLY

> 250G LAMB (OR MUTTON)

> 100G STREAKY BACON

> 500G FRESH GARLIC SAUSAGE, FOR FRYING (NOT SALAMI)

> 2 DUCK FILLETS/THIGHS (OR RABBIT)

> COCONUT OIL, FOR FRYING

> 2 RED ONIONS, FINELY SLICED

> 3 LARGE GARLIC CLOVES, CRUSHED

> 2 BAY LEAVES

> 500G HARICOT BEANS

> 1 HANDFUL THYME, FINELY CHOPPED

> 1 HANDFUL PARSLEY, FINELY CHOPPED

> 150G BREADCRUMBS (OPTIONAL)

<METHOD:>

Preheat the oven to gas mark 180ºC.

Cut all the meat into equal sized pieces, and brown over a medium heat in the coconut oil. When fully cooked remove the meat from the pan and reserve to one side, keeping the fat.

Sweat the onion and garlic in the remaining fat over a medium heat, once golden, mix with the chopped meat.

Next in an ovenproof dish thats big enough to hold all the ingredients, first layer the bay leaves and then layer up the chopped meat and beans. On each layer season with the chopped herbs.

Add enough water to fill the casserole dish to the halfway mark and add to the oven. When a crust has formed on top of your dish, stir this in and return to the oven, repeat this two or three times. The whole process should take around 2 hours but if add the breadcrumbs halfway through the cooking process to speed it up.

Finally leave to cool a little then serve.

<DINNER>

HEALTHY FISH AND CHIPS*

<SERVES: 01>

❝ ANOTHER BRITISH CLASSIC AND ONE WHICH CAN BE VERY HEALTHY TOO. A LIGHT CRISPY SEEDED BATTER OVEN BAKED OR FLASH FRIED IN COCONUT OIL – COMBINED WITH OVEN ROASTED CHIPS AND MUSHY PEAS. DROPPING THE CHIPS MAKES THIS A LOW CARB OPTION AND SWITCHES IT INTO THE GREEN ZONE!

<NUTRITION:>

PER SERVING:

> 790 KCAL

> 60G PROTEIN

> 80G CARBOHYDRATE

> 26G FAT

<INGREDIENTS:>

> 1 X 250G LARGE COD FILLET

> SALT AND PEPPER, TO TASTE

> 1 EGG, BEATEN

> 2 TBSP PUMPKIN SEED FLOUR

> 1 TSP GOOSE FAT

> 200G PEAS

> LARGE SPRIG MINT

> 400G MAJESTY PURPLE POTATOES, CHIPPED

> 1 TBSP OLIVE OIL

> HOME-MADE KETCHUP, TO SERVE

<METHOD:>

Preheat the oven to 200°C.

Season the cod and brush with the egg before dipping into the pumpkin seed flour to coat the fish.

Heat the goose fat on a very high heat, sear the cod skin-side down for 5 minutes, then turn to sear the other side. The seed flour should catch to give a golden brown. slightly burnt crust. This will take 10 minutes on each side normally – check the fish is opaque throughout and no longer translucent before serving.

For the mushy peas, just add enough water to cover them and add in the large sprig of mint. Bring to the boil and simmer for approximately 15 minutes until softened. By this point there should still be some water left with the peas; mash the peas directly in the pan along with the remaining water.

For the chips, place the chipped potatoes on a baking tray that has been liberally sprinkled with sea salt and the olive oil. Bake in the oven for 25-30 minutes.

Serve the cod, chips and mushy peas with home-made ketchup.

KEDGEREE*

<SERVES: 02>

<NUTRITION:>

PER SERVING:

> 355 KCAL

> 35G PROTEIN

> 40G CARBOHYDRATE

> 6G FAT

❝ *A FORGOTTEN CLASSIC – CAN BE EATEN AT ANY TIME OF THE DAY OR NIGHT. A HIGH PROTEIN FEAST OF FLAVOUR – BRINGING TOGETHER MANY GREAT INGREDIENTS.*

<INGREDIENTS:>

> 40-45G CAMARGUE RED
  (OR WHITE BASMATI) RICE

> 3 GARLIC CLOVES, CHOPPED

> 1 ONION, CHOPPED

> 1 TBSP COCONUT OIL

> 200G PEAS

> 300G SMOKED HADDOCK

> 4 BAY LEAVES

> 1 HEAPED TSP TURMERIC

> 2 HEAPED TSP CURRY POWDER

> 2 EGGS

<METHOD:>

First start boiling the rice in a pan according to the packet instructions.

In a separate pan fry the garlic and onions in the coconut oil over a low heat until soft. After these have softened and browned add the peas.

Meanwhile poach the fish with the bay leaves until soft – this will take 15 minutes. Drain the water then flake into a bowl and set to one side.

Finally add the spices, rice and flaked fish to the garlic/onion/pea mixture and mix well. Keep the dish warm in an oven or covered dish until ready to serve.

Poach the eggs over a medium heat until the whites are opaque and serve on top of the rice and fish mixture.

"THE KEY HERE IS TO START ALL THREE PANS AT ROUGHLY THE SAME TIME. START YOUR RICE EARLY THEN THE ONIONS AND SPICES – FINALLY POACH THE FISH – THIS GIVES EVERYTHING ENOUGH TIME TO COOK."
<MATT LOVELL>

<DINNER>

SEAFOOD PAELLA*

<SERVES: 02>

<NUTRITION:>

PER SERVING:

> 340 KCAL

> 30G PROTEIN

> 37G CARBOHYDRATE

> 8G FAT

WHO WOULD HAVE THOUGHT YOU CAN MAKE SO MANY DELICIOUS DISHES JUST BY CHANGING THE INGREDIENTS? YOU CAN MIX THIS UP TO INCLUDE OTHER MEATS, EXTRA SEAFOOD AND ALSO WHOLE PRAWNS OR LANGOUSTINES FOR EXTRA VISUAL EFFECT.

<INGREDIENTS:>

> 1 TBSP COCONUT OIL

> 4 GARLIC CLOVES, CHOPPED

> 1 ONION, CHOPPED

> 1 PEPPER, CHOPPED

> 90G PAELLA RICE

> SAFFRON, TO TASTE

> 1 HEAPED TSP TURMERIC

> 570ML CHICKEN STOCK

> 1 X 300G PACKET MIXED SEAFOOD

> 200G PEAS

> 1 LEMON, QUARTERED

<METHOD:>

Add the oil to a pan and fry the garlic, onion and pepper over a medium heat until soft, then add the rice and cook for 2 minutes.

Add the saffron and turmeric to the rice and then begin adding the stock. Continue cooking until the rice is soft – around 25-30 minutes.

Add the seafood and peas and cook through.

Serve with the lemon.

QUINOA LEEK RED RICE AND BROAD BEAN RISOTTO*

<SERVES: 03>

IT SOUNDS A CRAZY MEDLEY AND FRANKLY – IT IS, BUT FOR ANY VEGETARIANS THIS HOTPOT OF FUNCTIONAL INGREDIENTS. EXCELLENT PROTEIN SOURCES FROM QUINOA AND BROAD BEANS MEANS AN ARRAY OF AMINO ACIDS IS AVAILABLE TO THE PROTEIN-CONSCIOUS CONSUMER. AN EXCELLENT LOW-FAT HIGH-FIBRE CARB RECOVERY MEAL TO BOOT – GREAT ON ITS OWN OR A PERFECT ACCOMPANIMENT WITH A STEAK OR SALMON FILLET.

<NUTRITION:>

PER SERVING:

> 285 KCAL

> 11G PROTEIN

> 48G CARBOHYDRATE

> 5G FAT

<INGREDIENTS:>

> 4 GARLIC CLOVES, CHOPPED

> 1 RED ONION, CHOPPED

> 2 LEEKS, TRIMMED AND CHOPPED

> OLIVE OIL, FOR FRYING

> 90G RED RICE

> 90G QUINOA

> 500-750ML CHICKEN STOCK

> 200G BROAD BEANS

<METHOD:>

Fry the garlic, onion and leeks in a little olive oil over a low heat until soft. Add the rice and quinoa and fry for 10 minutes.

Gradually add enough stock to cover, put a lid on and cook for 30 minutes until cooked through.

Periodically check the stock and add more as necessary so it doesn't boil dry.

Once the rice and quinoa are cooked add the broad beans, heating them through before serving.

< DINNER >

HOME-MADE BURGERS AND RED CABBAGE SALAD*

<SERVES: 04>

<NUTRITION:>

PER SERVING:

> 400 KCAL

> 30G PROTEIN

> 3G CARBOHYDRATE

> 30G FAT

" A POWERHOUSE OF A MEAL – THE PATTIES CAN BE REINFORCED WITH ADDITIONAL SPICES AND MAYBE EVEN SOME LINSEEDS TO CREATE BURGERS WITH DIFFERENT THEMES. BLOOD-THINNING SPICES AND HERBS ROUND OFF THIS POWERHOUSE OF A SALAD NICELY. PERFECT EATEN AS AN ACCOMPANIMENT OR ALONE AS A MEAL OR STARTER.

<INGREDIENTS:>

> 500G ORGANIC LEAN STEAK MINCE

> 1 EGG YOLK

> 2 DSP PESTO

> 1 TSP CAJUN SPICES

> 1 GARLIC CLOVES, FINELY CHOPPED

> SALT AND PEPPER, TO TASTE

> SEED FLOUR (SESAME SEED FLOUR, LINSEED FLOUR OR SPELT FLOUR), TO BIND

> ½ RED CABBAGE, FINELY CHOPPED

> 2 CARROTS, VERY THINLY SLICED

> 2 SMALL HANDFUL OF WALNUTS

> 2 SMALL HANDFUL OF RAISINS

> 4 TBSP SESAME OIL

> 2 TBSP TERIYAKI MARINADE

> 4 TBSP BALSAMIC VINEGAR

> 4 TSP SOY SAUCE

> 2 DSP SUNDRIED TOMATOES, CHOPPED

<METHOD:>

Combine all the ingredients but the flour and mix with your hands.

Add enough flour to dry out the mixture and stop it sticking.

Form into patties and grill at a high temperature for 8 minutes each side.

Meanwhile mix together the cabbage, carrot, walnuts and raisins in a bowl.

In a jar with a lid on shake together the remaining dressing ingredients, when fully mixed drizzle over the salad and serve together with the burgers.

ALTERNATIVE:

You can enjoy this salad on its own, it's still a green dish and the stats are as follows: 200 KCAL, 5G PROTEIN, 23G CHO, 10G FAT per serving.

< DINNER >

BEEF AND BROAD BEANS*

<SERVES: 04>

<NUTRITION:>

PER SERVING:

> 270 KCAL

> 30G PROTEIN

> 13G CARBOHYDRATE

> 11G FAT

> THESE PAN-BASED DISHES ARE GOOD FOR TIRED PEOPLE COMING IN FROM A LONG DAY AS THEY ARE SO QUICK. ALWAYS A PROTEIN AND VEGETABLE 50:50 COMBINATION WITH ADDED SPICES AND GARLIC – THEY ALSO PACK A NUTRIENT-DENSE RECOVERY PUNCH WITH A LOW-GI AND HIGH FIBRE CONTENT. BROADS BEANS ALSO CONTAIN A HIGH LEVEL OF NATURALLY OCCURRING L-DOPA – WHICH CAN HELP MOTIVATION AND GROWTH HORMONE RELEASE.

<INGREDIENTS:>

> 3 GARLIC CLOVES, CHOPPED

> 1 TBSP COCONUT OIL

> 500G EXTRA LEAN ORGANIC STEAK MINCE

> 250G FROZEN BROAD BEANS

> 1 SMALL HANDFUL CHOPPED CHIVES

> 1 SPRIG THYME

> SALT AND PEPPER, TO TASTE

> STOCK, AS NEEDED

<METHOD:>

Fry the garlic in the coconut oil, add the mince and brown, then add the broad beans straight from frozen.

Add the chives and thyme, and keep moving over a low heat to draw out some liquid.

Season with salt and pepper, add a little stock if desired and heat through.

<DINNER>

BEEF STEW*

<SERVES: 02>

<NUTRITION:>

PER SERVING:

> 195 KCAL

> 24G PROTEIN

> 38G CARBOHYDRATE

> 6G FAT

> SLOW COOKING STEWS ARE EASY TO PREPARE AND IF YOU GET A SLOW COOKER YOU CAN LEAVE THESE ON A LOW SETTING ALL DAY TO BE READY FOR WHEN YOU GET HOME, A LITTLE PREPARATION TIME IN THE MORNING AND YOU'LL BE HOME TO A HEARTY STEW WITH ZERO COOKING TO DO. KEEPING THE STARCHY COMPONENT OUT OF DISHES IS SOMETHING YOU'LL BECOMING FAMILIAR WITH – SIMPLY SERVE THE STEW IN A BOWL AND EAT. NO NEED FOR RICE, POTATOES OR OTHER STARCHES AS THIS STEW USES PEARL BARLEY, WHICH CAN BE LEFT OUT IF YOU WANT THE LOWER CARB CONTENT.

<INGREDIENTS:>

> 350G BEEF BRISKET

> 1 ONION, CHOPPED

> 1 GARLIC CLOVE, CHOPPED

> 1 SMALL GLASS RED WINE

> 500ML GOOD BEEF STOCK

> 1 SPRIG THYME

> 1 BAY LEAF

> 40G PEARL BARLEY (OR QUINOA)

> 300G SWEDE AND CARROT, DICED

> 2 LARGE BEETROOTS

> 1 HANDFUL JUNIPER BERRIES

<METHOD:>

In a large pan heat the brisket gradually over a low heat to release the oils and brown the meat.

Gently turn up the heat and add the onion and garlic into the pan so that they cook in the meat juices.

Add the wine to the hot pan and reduce to two-thirds. Add the stock, thyme, bay leaf, pearl barley and vegetables into the pan and then simmer over a low heat for 30 minutes.

ALTERNATIVES:

Use other root vegetables like beetroot instead of swede and carrot.

<DINNER>

RABBIT WITH THYME AND COURGETTES*

<SERVES: 02>

<NUTRITION:>

PER SERVING:

> 260 KCAL

> 40G PROTEIN

> 14G CARBOHYDRATE

> 5G FAT

> **I'M REALLY INTO WILD GAME – IT'S LEANER, TENDS TO EAT WHAT IT SHOULD DO AND IS QUITE CHEAP TO PICK UP IF YOU KNOW A GOOD LOCAL BUTCHER OR POACHER. RABBIT ALSO GAINS LEAN WEIGHT ON ONE-SIXTH OF THE FOOD A COW NEEDS SO ENVIRONMENTALLY IT'S A GOOD CHOICE. HEALTH-WISE IT'S A LEAN SOURCE OF HIGH QUALITY PROTEIN WITH A CHICKEN TYPE CONSISTENCY.**

<INGREDIENTS:>

> 1 SMALL ONION, CHOPPED

> 30G FENNEL, CHOPPED

> 3 LARGE COURGETTES

> OLIVE OIL, FOR FRYING

> SEASONED FLOUR, FOR COATING

> 200G WILD RABBIT, CUT INTO EQUAL SIZE PORTIONS

> 1 LARGE GLASS WHITE WINE (OR WHITE VERMOUTH)

> 150ML GOOD QUALITY CHICKEN STOCK

> ½ A MEDIUM-SIZED BUNCH TARRAGON

> 1 BUNCH SAGE

> 1 LARGE HANDFUL THYME

> 4 CLOVES GARLIC, CRUSHED

> 2 COURGETTES, ROUGHLY CHOPPED

<METHOD:>

Brown the onion, garlic and fennel in the olive oil.

Place the seasoned flour and rabbit pieces in a plastic bag, then shake the bag gently to coat the rabbit.

Add the rabbit to the onions, oil and fennel, and brown. Add the liquids and herbs, beans and courgettes and simmer over a medium heat for 1-2 hours until cooked.

<QUICK TIP>

HOW TO CORE A PEPPER*

<1> CHOP THE BOTTOM OFF THE PEPPER – THIS IS THE END AWAY FROM THE STALK – TO GIVE A STABLE BASE.

<2> MAKE AN INCISION AT THE TOP AND CUT AROUND A CENTIMETRE AROUND THE STALK.

<3> REMOVE THE CORE, ENSURING THAT THE CORE COMES OUT WITH ALL THE SEEDS INTACT.

<4> THE PEPPER IS NOW READY FOR CHOPPING AS YOU WISH.

1.

2.

3.

4.

<PALM SIZED PLAN>

<DINNER>

THAI CHICKEN CURRY*

<SERVES: 01>

<NUTRITION:>

PER SERVING:

> 450 KCAL

> 40G PROTEIN

> 14G CARBOHYDRATE

> 27G FAT

COCONUT MILK WITH ITS MCTS AND LAURIC ACID HAS THE ABILITY TO PROVIDE INSTANT ENERGY AND IMMUNE ENHANCEMENT. THE THAI SPICE MIX ADDS BLOOD THINNING AND ADDITIONAL IMMUNE SUPPORT. THE DISH IS FILLING AND OVER SPILLING WITH VEGETABLES, THE CHICKEN BREAST KEEPS YOUR PROTEIN COMPONENT AND YOU CAN ADD RICE IF YOU WANT TO UP THE CARBOHYDRATE CONTENT OF THIS DISH.

<INGREDIENTS:>

> ½ ONION, CHOPPED

> ½ GARLIC CLOVE, CHOPPED

> 1 TSP GALANGAL

> 10G CASHEW NUTS

> 1 GREEN CHILLI, CHOPPED

> 1 HANDFUL FRESH CORIANDER

> HANDFUL THAI BASIL

> 1 TSP PALM SUGAR

> 1 CHICKEN BREAST, CHOPPED

> ⅛ TSP SHRIMP PASTE

> 1 TSP TAMARIND PASTE

> 1 TSP FISH SAUCE

> 200ML COCONUT MILK

> 1 TSP COCONUT OIL

<METHOD:>

Soften the onion and garlic over a low heat. Add the galangal, chilli, coriander, Thai basil and sugar then add the chicken until cooked through.

Add the remaining ingredients and simmer over a low heat for 20 minutes.

ALTERNATIVES:

You can easily make Thai red curry, just replace the green chilli with 1 red chili with 1 tbsp tomato purée, ½ tbsp ground cumin and 1 tsp ground coriander. To make a beef version replace the chicken with 200g lean beed mince.

Vegetarians can replace the chicken/beef with Brussels sprouts or broad beans.

< DINNER >

CHORIZO CHICKEN AND CHICKPEAS IN A PAN*

<SERVES: 02>

THIS CLASSIC MIXTURE TAKES 20 MINUTES FROM START TO FINISH, AS WELL AS BEING HIGH IN PROTEIN, FIBRE AND MONO-UNSATURATED FATS. THIS DISH CAN TAKE A LOT OF ADDITIONAL SPICES IF YOU LIKE IT HOT.

<NUTRITION:>

PER SERVING:

> 575 KCAL

> 45G PROTEIN

> 25G CARBOHYDRATE

> 33G FAT

<INGREDIENTS:>

> 4 GARLIC CLOVES, CHOPPED

> 1 CHICKEN BREAST, CHOPPED

> 2 CHORIZO SAUSAGES, CHOPPED

> OLIVE OIL, FOR FRYING

> 1 RED ONION, DICED

> 1 X 440G TIN CHICKPEAS

> 1 CHICKEN STOCK CUBE

> 10 CHERRY TOMATOES (OR ½ NORMAL SIZED TOMATO)

> 3 BAY LEAVES

> SALT AND PEPPER, TO TASTE

<METHOD:>

Fry on low heat the garlic, chicken and chorizo in olive oil until cooked through, add the onion and cook until soft.

Stir in the chickpeas and chicken stock cube, finally adding the tomatoes and cooking with the bay leaves for 10-15 minutes.

Season with salt and pepper just before serving.

< DINNER >

CHICKEN IN WHITE WINE AND MUSHROOM SAUCE*

<SERVES: 02>

<NUTRITION:>

PER SERVING:

> 550 KCAL

> 40G PROTEIN

> 30G CARBOHYDRATE

> 30G FAT

❝ *SHIITAKE MUSHROOMS ADD AN IMMUNE BOOSTING COMPONENT TO THIS MEAL WHICH CAN BE EASILY UPGRADED TO A HIGH ENERGY FEED WITH THE ADDITION OF SOME BASMATI OR OTHER STYLE RICE OR CARBOHYDRATE. AN EASY ONE TO ENJOY WITH CREAMY ADDITIONS SUCH AS CREAM OR SOUR CREAM TOO IF YOU ARE ENTERTAINING OR EATING OFF PLAN.*

<INGREDIENTS:>

> 3 GARLIC CLOVES, CHOPPED

> 1 TBSP OLIVE OIL

> 4 SMALL CHICKEN THIGHS

> 250ML WHITE WINE

> 400G SHIITAKE MUSHROOMS

> 1 DSP FRESH MIXED HERBS

> 250ML CREME FRAICHE

> SEASONING, TO TASTE

<METHOD:>

Fry the garlic in the oil in a pan over a medium heat until soft, then add the chicken to seal and brown off – this will take approximately 7 minutes each side.

Add the wine and mushrooms and cover and cook for 20 minutes.

To serve, add the herbs and crème fraîche, and season to taste.

POMEGRANATE PORK WITH SLOW-ROASTED SPICED RED CABBAGE*

<SERVES: 06>

ANOTHER FEAST OF FLAVOUR COMBINING DEEP PURPLES AND REDS IN A DELICIOUS AND JUICY LEAN PORK DISH. POMEGRANATES CONTAIN MASSIVE LEVELS OF PROTECTIVE NUTRIENTS, SLOWING PROSTATE SPECIFIC ANTIGEN INCREASES, AND POSSIBLY HELPING WITH CHOLESTEROL LEVELS TOO. BEWARE DRINKING TOO MUCH JUICE THOUGH, AS IT CONTAINS A LOT OF SUGAR.

<NUTRITION:>

PER SERVING:

> 525 KCAL

> 42G PROTEIN

> 11G CARBOHYDRATE

> 35G FAT

<INGREDIENTS:>

> 5 GARLIC CLOVES, CHOPPED

> 1 GINGER BULB, FINELY CHOPPED

> 2 TBSP OLIVE OIL

> 5 JUNIPER BERRIES

> 2 TSP CORIANDER SEEDS (OR CORIANDER POWDER)

> SALT AND PEPPER, TO TASTE

> 1 X 1KG PORK LOIN

> 2 POMEGRANATES

> 1½ RED CABBAGE, FINELY CHOPPED

> 1 TBSP BUTTER

> 1 LARGE PINCH GROUND NUTMEG

<METHOD:>

Blend the garlic, ginger, olive oil, juniper berries, coriander seeds/powder and salt and pepper into a paste. Strip the loin of any tough sinew, then score it deeply with a sharp knife and spread the paste over the meat.

Preheat the oven to 200ºC. Wrap the whole loin tightly in foil, adding the seeds of one of the pomegranates and roast for 40 minutes.

Steam the cabbage with the butter and nutmeg over a low heat for 25-30 minutes taking care not to burn the mixture.

After 40 minutes, remove the pork from the oven and allow it to rest for 10 minutes before slicing thinly.

Serve with the fresh seeds of the remaining pomegranate and cabbage.

< DINNER >

HONEY AND CLOVE ROASTED GAMMON WITH ROASTED VEGETABLES*

<SERVES: 06>

A REALLY NICE WAY TO COOK A ROAST SURROUNDED WITH SWEET CARROTS, ONIONS, GARLIC AND ANYTHING ELSE YOU MIGHT FIND IN THE CUPBOARD. THE JUICES OF THE HAM WILL HELP COOK THE VEGETABLES AND THE CLOVES AND HONEY INFUSES THE WHOLE DISH ADDING PROTECTIVE FACTORS AND A UNIQUE TASTE.

<NUTRITION:>

PER SERVING:

> 70 KCAL

> 2G PROTEIN

> 9G CARBOHYDRATE

> 3G FAT

<INGREDIENTS:>

> 20 CLOVES

> 1 X 2KG SMOKED GAMMON JOINT

> 20 CHANTERELLE CARROTS

> 2 MEDIUM RED ONIONS, ROUGHLY CHOPPED

> 5 GARLIC CLOVES, UNPEELED

> 1 TBSP OLIVE OIL

> 2 DSP MANUKA HONEY

> ½ TSP SALT

> ¼ TSP PEPPER

> 2 TBSP FINELY CHOPPED FRESH PARSLEY, TO SERVE

> 100G SPINACH, CHOPPED AND FRESHLY STEAMED, TO SERVE

<METHOD:>

Remove any packaging on the gammon joint and tie once round with a piece of string. Press the cloves into the topside of the gammon and preheat the oven to 200ºC.

Place the gammon in a large oven dish, surround with the chanterelle carrots, red onions and whole garlic cloves. Coat the top of the gammon in honey, oil and season.

Bake uncovered in the oven at 200ºC for 40-45 minutes or until tender and baste occasionally with the juices.

Stir the parsley in to the juices before serving and serve with the freshly steamed chopped spinach.

< DINNER >

LAMB MEDALLIONS WITH TAHINI ROASTED VEGETABLES*

<SERVES: 02>

> I NORMALLY USE TAHINI FROM A POT – BUT IT'S EASY ENOUGH TO KNOCK UP IF YOU LIKE THAT SORT OF THING. AGAIN THE LAMB PROVIDES JUICES WHICH THE VEGETABLES COOK IN AND YOU CAN SERVE WITH MORE FRESHLY STEAMED VEGETABLES OR A FRESH SALAD IF YOU WANT THE DIFFERENCE IN TEXTURES. PREPARATION TIME IS MINIMAL – AROUND 5 MINUTES – AND IT'LL BAKE IN 30 MINUTES OR LESS IF YOU LIKE YOUR LAMB PINK IN THE MIDDLE. MINT SAUCE OR RED JELLY TOP THIS OFF PERFECTLY.

<NUTRITION:>

PER SERVING:

> 330 KCAL

> 40G PROTEIN

> 12G CARBOHYDRATE

> 14G FAT

<INGREDIENTS:>

> 2 TBSP SESAME SEEDS

> ½ TSP SESAME OIL

> ¼ TSP SALT

> 125ML TEPID WATER

> 6 LAMB MEDALLIONS, TRIMMED

> 1 TBSP OLIVE OIL

> 2 TBSP TAHINI (SEE RECIPE ABOVE)

> 2 TSP CIDER VINEGAR

> 1 TSP HONEY

> SALT AND PEPPER, TO TASTE

> 4 CELERY STICKS, CHOPPED

> 4 CARROTS, CHOPPED

> 4-5 BROCCOLI SPEARS

> 2 MEDIUM COURGETTES, CHOPPED

> 2 MEDIUM ONIONS, CHOPPED

> 1 PINCH MIXED HERBS

> 6 GARLIC CLOVES, UNPEELED

<METHOD:>

Preheat the oven to 180°C.

For the tahini, blend the sesame seeds in a blender until smooth, then add the sesame oil and salt. While blending add the water in a very slow, steady stream and blend until smooth.

In a small bowl, combine the olive oil, tahini, vinegar, honey, salt and pepper. Drizzle over the vegetables and toss to coat. Place in the oven and bake with the lamb in a separate dish for 30 minutes.

Serve together with the roasted vegetables.

<DINNER>

MOROCCAN LAMB STEW*

<SERVES: 04>

> THIS CHEEKY, SPICY STEW FOLLOWS ON THE THEME OF COOKING IN ONE POT TO EAT FROM ONE BOWL, NO NEED TO ADD EXTRA STARCHY CARBS, THIS DISH IS FILLING AND NUTRITIOUS. YOU CAN ALSO USE THE SHEPHERD'S PIE MINCED LAMB MIX TO CONVERT INTO A STEW IF YOU WISH AND A SLOW COOKER IS AN EASY WAY TO GET THE FLAVOURS FLOWING AND THE LAMB NICE AND TENDER. LAMB NECK FILLETS ARE PERFECT FOR THIS TYPE OF STEW.

<NUTRITION:>

PER SERVING:

> 365 KCAL

> 33G PROTEIN

> 18G CARBOHYDRATE

> 18G FAT

<INGREDIENTS:>

> 400G LAMB NECK FILLETS, DICED

> COCONUT OIL, FOR FRYING

> 2 GARLIC CLOVES, CHOPPED

> 3 ONIONS

> 1 TSP CHILLI

> 1 TSP CORIANDER POWDER

> 1 TSP CUMIN

> 1 TSP CINNAMON

> 1 X 440G CAN CHERRY TOMATOES

> 500ML STOCK

> 2 LARGE CARROTS, SLICED

> 1 X 410G CAN COOKED GREEN LENTILS

> 4 BAY LEAVES

> 1 WHOLE LEMON, JUICE AND RIND

<METHOD:>

Dice the lamb into medallions and fry in the coconut oil over a medium heat.

Add the garlic, onions and spices and stir until the onions soften.

Stir in the tomatoes, stock, carrots, lentils and bay leaves. Simmer for 20 minute or until the lamb is cooked.

Drizzle lemon juice in and zest just before serving.

CHINESE SESAME LIVER STIR-FRY*

<SERVES: 03>

<NUTRITION:>

PER SERVING:

> 370 KCAL

> 38G PROTEIN

> 7G CARBOHYDRATE

> 21G FAT

> LIVER HAS MANY HEALTH GIVING BENEFITS AND HEAPS OF ESSENTIAL VITAMINS AND NUTRIENTS – BE CAREFUL IF YOU ARE PREGNANT OR INTENDING TO BECOME SO – AS THE HIGH LEVELS OF VITAMIN A SHOULD BE MODERATED AT THIS TIME. LIVER CONTAINS ABUNDANT IRON AND BLOOD BUILDING EFFECTS, AND IN CHINESE MEDICINE EATING THE ORGANS OF ANIMALS RESTORES THE MATCHING ORGAN IN HUMANS – THERE MAY BE SOME TRUTH IN THIS.

<INGREDIENTS:>

> 450G LAMB'S LIVER, SLICED

> 1 EGG, BEATEN

> 2 TSP CHINESE FIVE SPICE

> 20G SESAME SEEDS

> 1 GINGER BULB, SLICED

> 1 TSP SESAME OIL

> 100G BEAN SPROUTS

> 1 SMALL CARROT, SLICED THINLY

> 2 LARGE SPRING GREEN LEAVES, FINELY SHREDDED

> 50G BAMBOO SHOOTS

> 40G WATER CHESTNUTS, SLICED

> 1 SMALL BOK-CHOI

> 1 DSP SOY SAUCE

> 1 DSP SHERRY VINEGAR

> A DRIZZLE OF MOLASSES

<METHOD:>

Prepare the liver by mixing with the beaten egg and five spice. Then dip the slices in sesame seeds to coat them.

Over a very high heat, stir-fry the ginger and the liver slices, and remove from pan when the liver is crispy on the outside, but still pink in the middle.

Stir-fry the vegetables in the same pan for 5 minutes, then return the liver to the pan.

Season with the soy-sauce, sherry vinegar and a drizzle of molasses.

< DINNER >

SEAFOOD STIR-FRY*

<SERVES: 02>

<NUTRITION:>

PER SERVING:

> 230 KCAL

> 24G PROTEIN

> 20G CARBOHYDRATE

> 6G FAT

" *HERE'S ANOTHER SIMPLE WAY TO GET LOTS OF QUALITY LOW-FAT MINERAL RICH SEAFOODS, CHINESE FIVE-SPICE MIX AND CRISPY VEGETABLES. ADD OR TAKE AWAY NOODLES TO CHANGE THIS TO A GREEN DISH. EASY.*

<INGREDIENTS:>

> 1 TSP SESAME OIL

> 200G SHIITAKE MUSHROOMS

> ½ RED PEPPER, CHOPPED

> 1 CARROT, CHOPPED

> 1 RED ONION, CHOPPED

> 60G WHITE CABBAGE, SHREDDED

> 60G BEANSPROUTS

> 1 GARLIC CLOVE

> 1 GINGER BULB

> 4 RAW CHILLI

> 5 TSP CHINESE FIVE-SPICE

> 100ML PINEAPPLE JUICE

> 1 TBSP FISH SAUCE

> 2 DSP OYSTER SAUCE

> 1 TSP PEANUT BUTTER

> 300G MIXED FROZEN SEAFOOD

> 2 NESTS EGG NOODLES

> CORIANDER, TO SERVE

<METHOD:>

Heat up the sesame oil in a wok on a medium heat. Add the vegetables and five-spice powder and stir-fry these for 5 minutes.

To this add the juice, sauces, peanut butter and seafood, and cook for several minutes on a high hear until the sauce has thickened and the seafood has cooked through or thawed out, this will normally take 4-5 minutes.

When cooked serve with noodles and garnish with fresh coriander.

ALTERNATIVES:

Other vegetables can be used such as fennel for variation.

< DINNER >

PAN-FRIED SCALLOPS AND BOK CHOY*

<SERVES: 01>

> **LIKE MOST CRUSTACEANS SCALLOPS ARE LOW IN FAT AND HIGH IN MINERALS. THEY ARE ALSO REALLY HIGH IN TRYPTOPHAN, AN AMINO WHICH MAKE YOU FEEL GOOD. BOK CHOY IS A MEMBER OF THE CABBAGE FAMILY, A VEGETABLE KNOWN FOR ITS ANTI-MUTAGENIC EFFECTS. THESE VEGETABLES SHOULD BE A BACKBONE OF YOUR DAILY FOOD INTAKE. ONCE YOU GET THE HANG OF THESE STIR FRYS THEY BECOME REALLY QUICK AND EASY TO PREPARE.**

<INGREDIENTS:>

> BUTTER, FOR FRYING

> 1 GARLIC CLOVE, CRUSHED

> 6 SCALLOPS

> SALT AND PEPPER, TO TASTE

> 2 BOK CHOY, SLICED LENGTHWAYS OR QUARTERED

> 1 SPLASH WHITE WINE

> 1 TBSP OYSTER SAUCE

<METHOD:>

Melt the butter in a pan and add the garlic, then gently pan-fry the scallops and season well with salt and pepper.

Cook on a low heat for approximately 5 minutes on one side, then turn and cook for a further 2 minutes. The scallops should be slightly browned on the outside but only just cooked in the middle.

Remove from the pan and use the same pan with the scallop juices in it to stir-fry the bok choy on a medium heat for 2-5 minutes.

Add a splash of white wine to deglaze the pan, then add the oyster sauce; cook until the liquid has reduced, then serve as pictured.

<DINNER>

MULLET KALE AND BÉCHAMEL SAUCE*

<SERVES: 03>

<NUTRITION:>

PER SERVING:

> 420 KCAL

> 35G PROTEIN

> 15G CARBOHYDRATE

> 25G FAT

" FISH AND GREENS IS ONE OF THE BACKBONE MEALS FOR OPTIMUM BODY COMPOSITION AND THIS DISH SHOWS YOU CAN ENJOY THESE TYPES OF FOOD WITHOUT RELINQUISHING ON FLAVOUR OR SATISFACTION. KALE SCORES TOP OF THE NUTRIENT DENSITY TABLES AND EXTRA LEMON JUICE AND GARLIC FINISH THE FUNCTIONAL NATURE OF THIS DISH OFF NICELY.

<INGREDIENTS:>

> 400G FRESH MULLET

> 1 LEMON, QUARTERED

> 4 GARLIC CLOVES, CHOPPED

> 1 TBSP OLIVE OIL

> 1 X 200G PACKET OF KALE

> 1 DSP BUTTER

> 1 TBSP FLOUR

> 120ML MILK

> 1 HANDFUL DILL

> CHEESE, TO TASTE

<METHOD:>

Pan-fry the mullet in the olive oil with the lemon quarters and garlic over a medium heat for 8-10 minutes each side. Place a lid on the pan so the fish is half-fried and half-steamed.

Steam the kale in a separate pan until tender – normally 10-15 minutes.

While this is steaming make the béchamel sauce. Mix together the butter and flour to make a paste over a low heat. Add to this the milk, dill and a little cheese as desired, stirring continuously over a medium heat for around 7-10 minutes.

Serve the fish on top of the kale and cover with the sauce.

POLLOCK WITH BLACK OLIVE SAUCE*

<SERVES: 01>

FISH IN FOIL IS A SIMPLE ALL-IN-ONE METHOD OF COOKING FISH AND VEGETABLES ALL AT ONCE. IT'S A GREAT TIME-SAVER AND THE OVEN STEAMING FOIL METHOD MAINTAINS LOTS OF FLAVOUR AND JUICINESS IN THE FISH.

<NUTRITION:>

PER SERVING:

> 300 KCAL

> 32G PROTEIN

> 20G CARBOHYDRATE

> 10G FAT

<INGREDIENTS:>

> 1 SMALL COURGETTE, CHOPPED

> 100G BROCCOLI

> 100G FINE GREEN BEANS

> 200G POLLOCK FILLET

> 1 DSP BLACK OLIVE PASTE/TAPENADE

> JUICE OF ½ LEMON

> 1 GARLIC CLOVE, PEELED AND FINELY CHOPPED

> ½ FRESH RED CHILLI, DESEEDED AND FINELY CHOPPED

> 1 SPRIG OF FRESH ROSEMARY

> 1 SMALL HANDFUL CAPERS

> SEA SALT, TO TASTE

> 1 TSP BALSAMIC VINEGAR

> 1 TSP EXTRA VIRGIN OLIVE OIL

<METHOD:>

Preheat the oven 190ºC.

Make a bed of courgette, broccoli and green beans for your fish. Lay the fish on the vegetables and spread over the olive paste.

Squeeze the lemon juice over the fish, then on top of the fish add the garlic, chilli, rosemary and capers to the top of the fish so the flavours infuse while cooking.

Drizzle the vinegar and olive oil and season with salt, then fold the foil to make a tight parcel. Ensure the parcel is tight with no gaps to stop the fish from drying out and not cooking properly.

Cook in the oven for 25 minutes.

BAKED SEA BASS WITH ROSEMARY*

<SERVES: 01>

FISH ROASTED IN FOIL IS AN EASY WAY TO PREPARE A HEALTHY AND DELICIOUS MEAL WHILE YOU CHILL OUT OR GET ON WITH SOME THINGS YOU'VE BEEN MEANING TO DO! MAKE SURE YOUR PARCEL IS COMPLETELY AIR-TIGHT AS THIS WILL AFFECT HOW WELL AND HOW FAST THE DISH WILL COOK.

<NUTRITION:>

PER SERVING:

> 280 KCAL

> 26G PROTEIN

> 6G CARBOHYDRATE

> 19G FAT

<INGREDIENTS:>

> 1 X 120G SEA BASS FILLET

> 100G BROCCOLI, BLANCHED

> ½ CELERY HEART, CHOPPED

> 1 GARLIC CLOVE, PEELED AND FINELY CHOPPED

> 1 SPRIG FRESH ROSEMARY

> 1 HANDFUL BLACK OLIVES, STONED AND CHOPPED

> 1 SMALL HANDFUL FRESH HERBS, FINELY CHOPPED

> JUICE OF ½ LEMON

> 1 TSP BALSAMIC VINEGAR

> 1 TSP EXTRA VIRGIN OLIVE OIL

> BLACK PEPPER, TO TASTE

<METHOD:>

Preheat the oven 190ºC.

Make a bed of broccoli and celery for your fish then lay the fish on the vegetables.

Squeeze the lemon juice over the fish, then on top of the fish add the garlic, rosemary, olives and herbs to the top of the fish so the flavours infuse while cooking.

Drizzle the vinegar and olive oil and season with pepper, then fold the foil to make a tight parcel. Ensure the parcel is tight with no gaps to stop the fish from drying out and not cooking properly.

Cook in the oven for 25 minutes.

<DESSERT>

IF A SWEET TOOTH IS YOUR DOWNFALL, THESE RECIPES WILL SATISFY YOUR CRAVINGS. THERE ARE ALSO BISCUIT

AND CEREAL BAR RECIPES FOR WHEN YOU'RE ON THE RUN OR NEED AN ENERGY BOOST AFTER THE GYM

<DESSERT>

APPLE CRUMBLE*

<SERVES: 01>

<NUTRITION:>

PER SERVING:

> 515 KCAL

> 6G PROTEIN

> 82G CARBOHYDRATE

> 18G FAT

APPLE CRUMBLE IS SO TASTY WHEN MADE WELL AND AN EXCELLENT COMFORT OR HIGH CARBOHYDRATE DISH. ADDING A LITTLE LOW FAT CREME FRAICHE ROUNDS THIS OFF NICELY. A GREAT WAY TO ENERGISE AND FEEL GOOD.

<INGREDIENTS: >

> 2 ORGANIC APPLES

> 1 TSP CINNAMON

> 1 DSP MANUKA HONEY

> 2 TBSP WATER

> 150G HOME-MADE MUESLI

> 1 DSP HONEY, WARMED

> 1 DSP COCONUT OIL

<METHOD:>

Preheat the oven to 180°C.

Chop the apples, then combine with the cinnamon, honey and water. Put the mixture into an oven-proof bowl.

To make the topping, mix the muesli together with the honey and coconut oil using your fingers. Pat down the crumble mixture on top of the apple mixture.

Bake in the oven for 35-40 minutes.

<DESSERT>

PISTACHIO CAKE*

<SERVES: 8>

> **I LOVE THIS DISH – WHEN YOU USE COCONUT OIL AND SWEETENER INSTEAD OF THE BUTTER AND SUGAR IT STARTS TO LOOK LIKE A LOW-CARB POWERHOUSE OF A CAKE! PISTACHIOS ARE A GOOD SOURCE OF COPPER, PHOSPHORUS, POTASSIUM, MAGNESIUM AND B6. THE NUTS DELIVER 30 VITAMINS, MINERALS AND PHYTONUTRIENTS, SO THEY HAVE A CONSIDERABLE POWER-PACKED PUNCH FROM A NUTRITIONAL STANDPOINT.**

<INGREDIENTS:>

> 200G PISTACHIOS

> 50G SPELT FLOUR

> 2 TBSP COCONUT OIL

> JUICE OF 1 LEMON

> 1 VANILLA BEAN

> 200G SWEETENER

> 4 EGGS

> 1 TSP LOW-FAT CREME FRAICHE, TO SERVE

<METHOD:>

Preheat the oven to 160ºC.

Blend the pistachios into the flour then combine all the remaining ingredients and mix together thoroughly.

Grease a 20cm cake tin with coconut oil or use baking paper.

Bake until golden brown and cooked through – the centre shouldn't be too moist for around 30-40 minutes.

Serve with a dollop of low-fat crème fraîche.

<DESSERT>

HEALTHY CHOCOLATE CHIP COOKIES*

<MAKES: 10 COOKIES>

<NUTRITION:>

PER SERVING:

> 235 KCAL

> 7G PROTEIN

> 17G CARBOHYDRATE

> 15G FAT

> *THE CONCEPT OF A COOKIE CAN BE HEALTHY – JUST TAKE OUT THE SUGAR AND REPLACE WITH A SWEET FIBRE, ADD IN SOME EXCELLENT DARK CHOCOLATE WITH A FUNKY TYPE OF FLOUR LIKE SPELT OR COCONUT AND YOU'VE GOT A BESPOKE COOKIE WHICH BEATS MAINSTREAM ONES ANY DAY OF THE WEEK. THE MORE FAT YOU ADD TO YOUR COOKIE MIXTURE THE CRISPIER IT'LL BECOME.*

<INGREDIENTS:>

> 3 EGGS

> 200G PUMPKIN SEED FLOUR, FRESHLY MADE

> 33ML COCONUT OIL

> 150G SWEETENER

> 150G FLOUR (RYE OR OTHER AS SUGGESTED ABOVE)

> 100G DARK CHOCOLATE, BROKEN

<METHOD:>

Preheat the oven to 180°C.

Mix all the ingredients together.

Dollop the mix into rounds approximately the size of a cookie on baking paper then put in the oven for 20-25 minutes.

Leave to cool and serve.

ALTERNATIVE:

For sweeter, stickier biscuits add around 75ml of honey and molasses.

"PERFECT FOR AFTERNOON TEA, AFTER A COLD DAY WALKING AROUND TOWN."
<MATT LOVELL>

<DESSERT>

ON-THE-RUN HOME-MADE HEALTHY BARS*

<MAKES: 15 BARS>

<NUTRITION:>

PER SERVING (PER BAR):

> 190 KCAL

> 10G PROTEIN

> 21G CARBOHYDRATE

> 7G FAT

> *YOU CAN SPEND A FORTUNE ON PROTEIN AND ENERGY BARS – AND SOMETIMES THESE COME IN REALLY HANDY. HOME-MADE BARS ARE EASY AND YOU CAN MAKE THEM LOWER OR HIGHER IN PROTEIN OR CARBS. SIMPLE PRINCIPLES, SOME GRAINS, SOME SEEDS, SOME PROTEIN POWDER AND FAT OR FRUIT TO HOLD THEM TOGETHER.*

<INGREDIENTS:>

> 75G JUMBO OATS

> 25G SUNFLOWER SEEDS

> 4 SCOOPS VANILLA WHEY PROTEIN POWDER

> 50G SPELT FLOUR

> 30G SLICED ALMONDS

> 2 TBSP GROUND FLAX SEED

> 25G DRIED BLUEBERRIES (OR TART CHERRIES)

> 25G GOOD QUALITY DARK CHOCOLATE, CHIPPED/GRATED (OR 1 DSP COCOA POWDER)

> WATER, AS NEEDED

> 2 TBSP FLAX-SEED OIL

> 3 TBSP PURE MAPLE SYRUP (OR 3 TBSP MOLASSES)

> 2 LARGE EGGS

<METHOD:>

Mix the dry ingredients and slowly add the water until the consistency of bread-dough.

Fold in the flax, maple syrup and the eggs until mixed through.

Spread on a baking sheet 2.5cm thick on grease proof paper or rice paper and bake for 20 minutes at 180°C.

Score when warm and then leave to cool before removing from the tray.

<DESSERT>

POACHED PEAR*

<SERVES: 01>

<NUTRITION:>

PER SERVING:

> 90 KCAL

> 1G PROTEIN

> 17G CARBOHYDRATE

> 0G FAT

" A HEALTHY DESSERT AND ONE YOUR GUESTS WILL NOT BE DISAPPOINTED WITH. BY ADDING 0% GREEK YOGHURT YOU CAN RAISE THE PROTEIN CONTENT NICELY – MAKING IT GREAT IF YOU FANCY A SWEET SNACK.

<INGREDIENTS:>

> 1 PEAR, HALVED AND STONED

> 375ML WHITE WINE

> 1 STAR ANISE

> 2 CLOVES

> 1 TSP GOOD VANILLA ESSENCE

> 1 TSP 0% FAT GREEK YOGHURT

> SAIGON CINNAMON, TO TASTE

<METHOD:>

Place the pear in a pan on a medium heat, pour the wine to just cover the pear, add the spices and vanilla essence.

Leave to simmer for approximately 20 minutes, so that the pear softens but does not begin to disintegrate.

Remove from the heat and serve with a dollop of 0% fat Greek yoghurt and a sprinkle of Saigon cinnamon.

<DESSERT>

SYLLABUB*

<SERVES: 06>

<NUTRITION:>

PER SERVING:

> 285 KCAL

> 06G PROTEIN

> 14G CARBOHYDRATE

> 20G FAT

THIS IS A RECOVERY DISH BUT IT'S ONE FOR AN 'OFF' DAY – IT'S BASICALLY AN ADVANCED MUSCLE-GAINING FORMULA. EGG WHITES, SUGAR, CREAM AND ALCOHOL MAKE A HIGH-CALORIE HIGH-INSULIN RAISING DISH WHICH IS DELICIOUS. YOU CAN TAKE THE CALORIES DOWN USING SWEETENER AND CREME FRAICHE INSTEAD OF NORMAL CREAM – BUT IT DOES CHANGE THE NATURE OF THE DISH. ADDITIONAL GINGER AND SPICES SUCH AS CINNAMON CAN BE ADDED TO ENHANCE THE FLAVOUR AND MEDICINAL PROPERTIES OF THIS DISH.

<INGREDIENTS:>

> 1 LEMON RIND, THINLY SLICED

> 4 TBSP LEMON JUICE

> 4 EGG WHITES

> 125ML WHITE (WINE OR SHERRY)

> 2 TBSP BRANDY

> 75G CASTER SUGAR (OR SWEETENER)

> 250ML CREAM (OR CREME FRAICHE), LIGHTLY WHIPPED

> GRATED NUTMEG, TO SERVE

<METHOD:>

Beat the egg whites until slightly stiff and combine the ingredients, finally stir in the sugar.

Use a blender to increase the thickness of the mixture without allowing it to become too thick.

<DESSERT>

RHUBARB FOOL *

<SERVES: 01>

<NUTRITION:>

PER SERVING:

> 185 KCAL

> 21G PROTEIN

> 25G CARBOHYDRATE

> 0G FAT

" ANOTHER HEALTHY WAY TO ENJOY SOMETHING SWEET – THE TARTNESS OF RHUBARB GOES REALLY WELL WITH THE CREAMINESS OF THE CREME FRAICHE WHILE THE BERRIES AND OTHER INGREDIENTS ADD VITAMIN C RICH NUTRIENTS.

<INGREDIENTS:>

> 2 TSP WATER

> 227G RHUBARB, FINELY CHOPPED

> A HANDFUL CRANBERRIES

> JUICE OF ½ A GRAPEFRUIT

> 1 DSP HONEY

> 1 SMALL POT CREME FRAICHE (OR LOW FAT YOGHURT)

> CINNAMON, TO SERVE

<METHOD:>

Put the water into a small pan, add the rhubarb, cranberries and the grapefruit juice.

Leave to simmer over a low heat until the mixture reduces and softens.

Take off the heat and add honey to taste.

Leave to cool, mix in the crème fraîche, sprinkle with cinnamon as desired and serve.

"THE CREME FRAICHE CAN BE EXCHANGED FOR 0% FAT GREEK YOGHURT IF YOU WANT A LOWER FAT, HIGHER PROTEIN OPTION."
<MATT LOVELL>

<DESSERT>

MANDARIN AND GINGER*

<SERVES: 01>

<NUTRITION:>

PER SERVING:

> 75 KCAL

> 1G PROTEIN

> 15G CARBOHYDRATE

> 0G FAT

 *SIMPLE DISHES ARE OFTEN THE BEST – AND THIS MAKES A NICE SNACK OR BREAKFAST. YOU CAN ADD LOW-FAT GREEK YOGHURT TO INCREASE THE PROTEIN CONTENT IF YOU WISH. CRYSTALLISED STEM GINGER IS ALSO A HEALTHY ALTERNATIVE TO MANY COMMERCIALLY AVAILABLE CONFECTIONERY PRODUCTS.*

<INGREDIENTS:>

> 2 MANDARINS

> 2 TSP COINTREAU

> 2 TSP CRYSTALLISED STEM GINGER, FINELY CHOPPED

> 1 TSP CREME FRAICHE

<METHOD:>

Slice the mandarins, combine with the Cointreau and ginger, add the crème fraîche and serve.

<DESSERT>

GREEN TEA ICE CREAM*

<SERVES: 04>

<NUTRITION:>

PER SERVING:

> 220 KCAL

> 36G PROTEIN

> 14G CARBOHYDRATE

> 2G FAT

" ANOTHER DESSERT WHICH IS REALLY GOOD FOR YOU. AS MATCHA CAN BE QUITE BITTER IT'S GOOD TO USE THE CHOCOLATE TO MASK AND BRING THE FLAVOURS TOGETHER – PLUS THIS TURNS THE WHOLE THING INTO A 'FLAVONOID' PARTY!

<INGREDIENTS:>

> 400G LOW-FAT FROZEN YOGHURT/PROTEIN ICE CREAM

> 3 TBSP MATCHA GREEN TEA POWDER

> BLUEBERRIES, TO SERVE

> 80% DARK CHOCOLATE, FINELY GRATED, TO TASTE

> FRESHLY GROUND NUTMEG, TO SERVE

<METHOD:>

Leave the frozen yoghurt/protein ice cream to soften and stir in the tea powder.

Serve with blueberries and finely grated dark chocolate, a dusting of nutmeg rounds this delicious healthy treat off nicely.

<DESSERT>

BAKED BANANAS AND MOLASSES*

<SERVES: 02>

ONE OF THE SIMPLEST AND MOST DELICIOUS DESSERTS AND THE DISH VIRTUALLY PREPARES ITSELF. THE MOLASSES ARE A POWERHOUSE OF SWEETNESS, MINERALS AND B-VITAMINS PLUS BANANAS CONTAIN DECENT LEVELS OF MINERALS SUCH AS MAGNESIUM AND POTASSIUM, GOOD FOR CELLULAR FUNCTION.

<NUTRITION:>

PER SERVING:

> 335 KCAL

> 4G PROTEIN

> 85G CARBOHYDRATE

> 0G FAT

<INGREDIENTS:>

> 3 BANANAS, PEELED AND CHOPPED

> 1 HEAPED TSP MOLASSES

<METHOD:>

Chop the bananas lengthways or in round slices.

Cover with the molasses, and bake in the oven at 150°C for 20 minutes or until bananas have softened and darkened slightly in colour.

Serve with reduced fat crème fraîche.

<DESSERT>

BERRY JELLY*

<SERVES: 04>

<NUTRITION:>

PER SERVING:

> 60 KCAL

> 2G PROTEIN

> 14G CARBOHYDRATE

> 0G FAT

 JELLY FROM PROPER GELATINE IS HIGH IN PROTEIN AND HELPS FORM STRONG BONES, NAILS, HAIR AND TEETH – IT'S ALSO GOT A ROLE TO PLAY IN HEALTHY JOINTS AND THE DIGESTIVE SYSTEM – ONE OF THE REASONS CHICKEN STOCK IS SO HEALTHY IS ITS HIGH GELATINE CONTENT. GELATINE ITSELF IS VERY SIMILAR IN STRUCTURE TO TYPE 2 COLLAGEN (CONNECTIVE TISSUE), WHICH IS AN IMPORTANT PART OF CARTILAGE.

<INGREDIENTS:>

> 100G REDCURRANTS

> 50G STRAWBERRIES

> 50G BLACKBERRIES

> 50G SUGAR

> 25G SWEETENER

> 1 GELATINE LEAF

<METHOD:>

Cook the berries gently over a low heat until broken down – this usually takes 5-10 minutes

then add the sugar and boil vigorously for 10 minutes.

Add the sweetener, gelatine and stir.

In four glasses add a handful of berries and then top with the warm gelatine mixture.

Leave to cool and then add to the fridge until set then serve.

PERFECT FOR THAT PROTEIN BOOST BEFORE EXERCISING — THESE NUTRIENT DENSE SHAKES ARE A GREAT WAY TO ADD A FOURTH MEAL TO YOUR DIET.

FOR THOSE LOOKING TO SLIM DOWN GREEN TEA IS KING — OFFERING A GREAT SOURCE OF ANTIOXIDANTS AND FAT BUSTING COMPONENTS!

<DRINK>

SMOOTHIES*

❝ PROTEIN SMOOTHIES – A GREAT WAY TO ENJOY A BALANCED NUTRITIONAL INTAKE WITHOUT HAVING A FULL MEAL. OVER THE FOLLOWING PAGES FIND A SELECTION OF RECIPES TO SUIT DIFFERENT TASTES, SIMPLY POP THE INGREDIENTS INTO A BLENDER AND BLITZ!

CHOCOLATE AND NUT SMOOTHIE*
<SERVES: 02>

STRAWBERRY COCONUT SMOOTHIE*
<SERVES: 01>

BERRY IMMUNE BOOSTER*
<SERVES: 01>

<NUTRITION:>

PER SERVING:

> 370 KCAL

> 33G PROTEIN

> 12G CARBOHYDRATE

> 20G FAT

<NUTRITION:>

PER SERVING:

> 358 KCAL

> 25G PROTEIN

> 30G CARBOHYDRATE

> 12G FAT

<NUTRITION:>

PER SERVING:

> 380 KCAL

> 31G PROTEIN

> 60G CARBOHYDRATE

> 2G FAT

<INGREDIENTS:>

> 2 SCOOPS CHOCOLATE WHEY PROTEIN POWDER

> 125G FAT-FREE COTTAGE CHEESE

> 1 TSP NATURAL PEANUT BUTTER

> 4 SQUARES ORGANIC DARK CHOCOLATE

> 1 SMALL HANDFUL ALMONDS

> 1 TSP MARMALADE

> 1 TSP LINSEEDS

> ½ TBSP LECITHIN GRANULES

> 150ML SKIMMED MILK

> 150ML WATER

<INGREDIENTS:>

> 1 LARGE HANDFUL FRESH STRAWBERRIES, CHOPPED

> 1 TSP COCONUT MILK

> 1 BANANA, CHOPPED

> 1 TSP NO ADDED SUGAR BLUEBERRY JAM

> 1 TSP HEMP SEED OIL

> 1 SCOOP STRAWBERRY FLAVOURED WHEY PROTEIN POWDER

> COCOA, TO SERVE

<INGREDIENTS:>

> 1 HANDFUL DRIED BLUEBERRIES

> 1 APPLE, CHOPPED

> 1 SCOOP STRAWBERRY-FLAVOURED WHEY PROTEIN POWDER

> 1 DSP NO ADDED SUGAR BLUEBERRY JAM

> 1 HANDFUL PRUNES

> 1 DSP LOW-FAT COTTAGE CHEESE

> 1 DSP NATURAL YOGHURT

> 150ML WATER

> 1 HANDFUL CRUNCHY GRANOLA (OR MUESLI), TO SERVE

SMOOTHIE RECIPES*

BERRY EXPLOSION*
<SERVES: 01>

COCONUTS*
<SERVES: 01>

STRAWBERRY CHEESECAKE*
<SERVES: 01>

MARATHON*
<SERVES: 01>

<NUTRITION:>

PER SERVING:

> 158 KCAL

> 21G PROTEIN

> 12.3G CARBOHYDRATE

> 2.6G FAT

<NUTRITION:>

PER SERVING:

> 356 KCAL

> 35.8G PROTEIN

> 28.1G CARBOHYDRATE

> 12G FAT

<NUTRITION:>

PER SERVING:

> 314 KCAL

> 36.75G PROTEIN

> 32.8G CARBOHYDRATE

> 4.35G FAT

<NUTRITION:>

PER SERVING:

> 357 KCAL

> 43.5G PROTEIN

> 26.3G CARBOHYDRATE

> 10G FAT

<INGREDIENTS:>

> 1 SCOOP VANILLA WHEY PROTEIN POWDER

> 2 HANDFUL MIXED BERRIES

> 1 TSP HONEY

> 1 TSP SPIRULINA

> 1 DSP LECITHIN GRANULES

> 250-300ML WATER (OR SKIMMED MILK)

<INGREDIENTS:>

> 1 SCOOP CHOCOLATE WHEY PROTEIN POWDER

> 250-300ML SKIMMED MILK

> 1 DSP LECITHIN GRANULES

> 1 TSP LINSEEDS

> 1 TSP COCONUT OIL

> 1 TSP PEANUT BUTTER

> 1 TSP COCOA POWDER

<INGREDIENTS:>

> 1 SCOOP STRAWBERRY WHEY PROTEIN POWDER

> 250-300ML SKIMMED MILK

> 1 TSP LOW-FAT COTTAGE CHEESE

> 1 HANDFUL STRAWBERRIES

> 1 TSP LOW-FAT SOUR CREAM

> 1 PINCH LEMON ZEST

<INGREDIENTS:>

> 2-3 SCOOPS CHOCOLATE WHEY PROTEIN POWDER

> 250-300ML SKIMMED MILK

> 50G LOW-FAT COTTAGE CHEESE

> 2 TSP NATURAL PEANUT BUTTER

> 1 TBSP LINSEEDS

> ½ TBSP LECITHIN GRANULES

"SIMPLY POP THE INGREDIENTS INTO A BLENDER AND BLITZ!"

<MATT LOVELL>

APPLE STRUDEL*
<SERVES: 01>

SEEDY SLICKSTER*
<SERVES: 01>

FARMHOUSE SMOOTHIE*
<SERVES: 01>

RICE PUDDING*
<SERVES: 01>

<NUTRITION:>

PER SERVING:

> 162 KCAL

> 21.6G PROTEIN

> 10.3G CARBOHYDRATE

> 4G FAT

<NUTRITION:>

PER SERVING:

> 167 KCAL

> 22.8G PROTEIN

> 3.8G CARBOHYDRATE

> 6.5G FAT

<NUTRITION:>

PER SERVING:

> 379 KCAL

> 36.8G PROTEIN

> 43.2G CARBOHYDRATE

> 8.1G FAT

<NUTRITION:>

PER SERVING:

> 257 KCAL

> 24.6G PROTEIN

> 24.3G CARBOHYDRATE

> 7G FAT

<INGREDIENTS:>

> 2-3 SCOOPS VANILLA WHEY PROTEIN POWDER

> 47G NATURAL UNSWEETENED APPLE SAUCE

> CINNAMON, AS DESIRED

> 300ML COLD WATER

> 1 TBSP LINSEEDS

> ½ TBSP LECITHIN GRANULES

<INGREDIENTS:>

> 2-3 SCOOPS CHOCOLATE WHEY PROTEIN POWDER

> 1 TSP NATURAL PEANUT BUTTER

> 300-400ML COLD WATER

> 1 TBSP LINSEEDS

> ½ TBSP LECITHIN GRANULES

<INGREDIENTS:>

> 50G UNFLAVORED OATMEAL

> 1-2 SCOOPS VANILLA WHEY PROTEIN POWDER

> 50-100G LOW-FAT COTTAGE CHEESE

> 400ML COLD WATER

> 1 TBSP LINSEEDS

> ½ TBSP LECITHIN GRANULES

<INGREDIENTS:>

> 2 SCOOPS VANILLA WHEY PROTEIN POWDER

> 2-3 TBSP SUGAR-FREE INSTANT RICE PUDDING

> 5 ICE CUBES

> 300-400ML COLD WATER

> 1 TBSP LINSEEDS

> ½ TBSP LECITHIN GRANULES

SMOOTHIE RECIPES*

BANANA SPLIT SHAKE*
<SERVES: 01>

BAR-BLITZ-VAH*
<SERVES: 01>

KEY LIME*
<SERVES: 01>

<NUTRITION:>

PER SERVING:

> 217 KCAL

> 22.4G PROTEIN

> 5.5G CARBOHYDRATE

> 4.2G FAT

<NUTRITION:>

PER SERVING:

> 257 KCAL

> 35.25G PROTEIN

> 13.3G CARBOHYDRATE

> 7G FAT

<NUTRITION:>

PER SERVING:

> 211 KCAL

> 22.7 PROTEIN

> 13.3G CARBOHYDRATE

> 7.1G FAT

<INGREDIENTS:>

> 2-3 SCOOPS VANILLA WHEY PROTEIN POWDER

> 100G BANANA, PINEAPPLE AND FRESH OR FROZEN STRAWBERRIES

> 300-400ML COLD WATER (OR SKIMMED MILK)

> 1 TBSP LINSEEDS

> ½ TBSP LECITHIN GRANULES

<INGREDIENTS:>

> 1 SCOOP WHEY PROTEIN POWDER

> 50G LOW FAT COTTAGE CHEESE

> ½ PROTEIN BAR

> 300-400ML COLD WATER (OR SKIMMED MILK)

> 1 TBSP LINSEEDS

> ½ TBSP LECITHIN GRANULES

<INGREDIENTS:>

> 2 SCOOPS WHEY PROTEIN POWDER

> 300-400ML COLD WATER (OR SKIMMED MILK)

> 2 TBSP FROZEN LIME JUICE

> 1 DIGESTIVE BISCUIT

> 3 ICE CUBES

> 1 TBSP LINSEEDS

> ½ TBSP LECITHIN GRANULES

"SIMPLY POP THE INGREDIENTS INTO A BLENDER AND BLITZ!"
<MATT LOVELL>

CARROT CAKE*
<SERVES: 01>

CHEAT DAY*
<SERVES: 01>

MATTEO'S ADDICTION FIGHTING SHAKE*
<SERVES: 01>

<NUTRITION:>

PER SERVING:

> 386 KCAL

> 18G PROTEIN

> 44.5G CARBOHYDRATE

> 23G FAT

<NUTRITION:>

PER SERVING:

> 569 KCAL

> 33G PROTEIN

> 37.5G CARBOHYDRATE

> 39G FAT

<NUTRITION:>

PER SERVING:

> 380 KCAL

> 31G PROTEIN

> 60G CARBOHYDRATE

> 2G FAT

<INGREDIENTS:>

> 1 SCOOP VANILLA WHEY PROTEIN POWDER

> 2 TBSP ALMOND BUTTER

> 1 LARGE CARROT, SLICED

> ½ APPLE, SLICED

> 1 TBSP LINSEEDS

> ½ TBSP LECITHIN GRANULES

<INGREDIENTS:>

> 1-2 SCOOPS CHOCOLATE WHEY PROTEIN POWDER

> 1TBSP LOW-FAT CREAM

> 1 DIGESTIVE BISCUIT, CRUSHED

> 1 SMALL FROZEN BANANA, SLICED

> 1 TBSP LINSEEDS

> ½ TBSP LECITHIN GRANULES

<INGREDIENTS:>

> 1 HANDFUL DRIED BLUEBERRIES

> 1 HANDFUL PRUNES

> 1 APPLE, CHOPPED

> 1 SCOOP STRAWBERRY WHEY PROTEIN POWDER

> 1 TBSP BLUEBERRIES

> 1 TBSP LOW-FAT COTTAGE CHEESE

> 1 TBSP NATURAL YOGHURT

> 150ML WATER

> 1 TSP GRANOLA/MUESLI, TO SERVE

<DRINK>

GINGER ZINGER*

<SERVES: 01>

<NUTRITION:>

PER SERVING:

> 95 KCAL

> 3G PROTEIN

> 21G CARBOHYDRATE

> 0G FAT

❝❝ GINGER ASSISTS DIGESTION AND MENTAL FOCUS – MAKING IT A GREAT WAY TO START THE DAY. THE GINGEROLS ALSO ACT AS POWERFUL ANTI-INFLAMMATORIES SO ARE GREAT FOR RECOVERY IN COMBATING MUSCLE SORENESS AND ACHING JOINTS.

<INGREDIENTS:>

> 1 APPLE, JUICED

> 1 LEMON, JUICED

> 1 KIWI, JUICED

> 1 LARGE BULB GINGER

<METHOD:>

Blend all the ingredients together in a juicer.

ALTERNATIVE:

You can also chop the ingredients to make a zingy fruit salad – just peel the skins off first.

"FOR A CHANGE YOU CAN ALSO USE CARROT OR PEAR INSTEAD OF APPLE."
<MATT LOVELL>

SELECTION OF TEAS*

OOLONG TEA

Some say oolong tea others say wulong tea, but both are sold as the weight-loss tea by diet websites. The slimming benefits are still in the research stage and results are imminent.

In the best-selling book *You, Staying Young* by Dr. Oz, of the Dr. Oz show and Michael Roizen M.D., studies show that oolong tea contains polyphenols. In fact, any green tea has a high content of polyphenols, which are chemicals with potent antioxidant properties even greater than vitamin C. Polyphenols have been shown to help improve metabolism of nutritional fat which helps to control body fat.

According to Dr. Oz and Dr. Roizen, "One study showed that those who drank two cups of [oolong tea] a day had two and a half times the calorie-burning rate of those who drank traditional green tea." The authors conclude that even though the research is in the early stages, the results are promising.

GREEN TEA

The health benefits of any tea, especially green tea, are good. Next to fish oils green tea is a wonder food. Drink it regularly – get a version you enjoy the taste of. The best product is matcha ceremonial green tea used in the Orient for thousands of years to improve mediation and meetings between people. Here's a list of what it does:

Calms the brain

Increases both GABA (A brain neurotransmitter which regulates rhythm and calmness) and Dopamine (A brain neurotransmitter which makes you feel happy)

Excellent for decision-making when under fire

Increases alpha-waves, seen in wakefulness where there is a relaxed and effortless alertness

Protects against most diseases

Burns fat

There's heaps of research supporting green tea's anti-cancer properties, anti-obesity and increased fat-burning effects!

GINSENG TEA

There's a mass of references on ginseng tea; it helps boost the immune system, energy, sexual stamina and athletic performance to name but a few.

HONEY AND GINGER

Ginger is a traditional remedy tea with many restorative components, especially if you add some Manuka honey and real lemon juice or even better the water from a whole unwaxed organic lemon which has been steeped and boiled for 20 minutes. The limonene from the skin has many powerful antioxidant benefits.

Manuka honey is high in antioxidants and has immune-boosting properties and natural wound-healing properties. It contains powerful, unique antibacterial properties in addition to its hydrogen peroxide scavenging activity. Hydrogen peroxide is a powerful free radical. Free radicals wreak havoc in the body if they are not 'quenched' through antioxidant intake.

Manuka honey is effective against a wide range of bacteria including the major wound-infecting bacteria and the stomach-ulcer causing bacteria Helicobacter pylori.

The New Zealand honey has a registered trademark, UMF®, so it cannot be misrepresented. The trademark number confirms the honey has a high antibacterial activity.

BITTER MELON TEA

Actually bitter melon itself is a useful culinary delight which has various benefits for digestive health and blood-glucose regulation. Because it can lower blood glucose it's best taken with meals or directly afterwards.

TURKISH TEA

This tea was recommended to me by one of my clients. She uses it to keep regular and it actually contains a nice blend of digestive and diuretic herbs. So useful for detox and good regular bowel movements.

AMERICAN GINSENG TEA

American ginseng has powerful immune-boosting properties. In fact there's a positive correlation between people who consume a lot of ginseng teas and a lower incidence of all type of cancer, although they didn't account for other variables. American ginseng tea is calming in nature so can be drunk later in the day unlike panax which is stimulating. In Chinese medicine American ginseng tea stimulates fluids in the body and acts as a yin tonic.

KUDZU

Kudzu is a type of starchy root which is claimed to have powerful cleansing abilities. It can help with alcohol detoxification. You can make a tea with kudzu with 1 teaspoon of kudzu stirred into hot water and lemon juice, adding a little soy sauce and ginger and allowing to steep for 5 minutes.

INDEX*

CRAB

> CRAB SALAD 76
> CRAB GUACAMOLE SALAD 80
> PRAWN COCKTAIL 82

CURRY

> THAI CHICKEN CURRY 156

DUCK

> CASSOULET 136

EGGS

> BEANS AND EGGS ON TOAST 26
> SCRAMBLED EGGS AND SMOKED SALMON
  ON TOAST 28
> HEALTHY BACON AND EGGS 30
> THREE EGG SPINACH OMELETTE 32
> TUNA AND CHILLI FRITTATA 34
> CHORIZO EGGS 36
> VEGETARIAN EGG AND ASPARAGUS PIZZA 104
> KEDGEREE 140

GAMMON

> HONEY AND CLOVE ROASTED GAMMON WITH
  ROASTED VEGETABLES 164

GINGER

> POT-ROASTED GUINEA FOWL IN GINGER
  WINE 122
> MANDARIN AND GINGER 198
> GINGER ZINGER 214

GREEN TEA

> GREEN TEA ICE CREAM 200
> SELECTION OF TEAS 216

GUINEA FOWL

> POT-ROASTED GUINEA FOWL IN GINGER
  WINE 122

HADDOCK

> KEDGEREE 140

HAM

> HAM BEETROOT TOMATO CARROT AND
  SAUERKRAUT SALAD 88
> HAM AND WATERCRESS SOUP 96

HARISSA

> SAUSAGE AND MASH WITH RED ONIONS
  AND HARISSA PASTE 128

HEALTHY BARS

> ON-THE-RUN HOME-MADE HEALTHY BARS 190

HUMOUS

> HUMOUS 46

ICE CREAM

> GREEN TEA ICE CREAM 200

JELLY

> BERRY JELLY 204

KALE

> MULLET KALE AND BECHAMEL SAUCE 176

LAMB

> HEALTHY SHEPHERD'S PIE 130
> SPICY MOROCCAN LAMB COUS COUS 134
> KEBAB AND BEAN DAHL 132
> CASSOULET 136
> LAMB MEDALLIONS WITH TAHINI ROASTED
  VEGETABLES 166
> MOROCCAN LAMB STEW 168

LIVER

> CHINESE SESAME LIVER STIR-FRY 170

MACKEREL

> MACKEREL PATE 66

MANDARIN

> MANDARIN AND GINGER 198

MOLASSES

> BAKED BANANAS AND MOLASSES 202

MUESLI

> HOME-MADE MUESLI 22

MULLET

> MULLET KALE AND BECHAMEL SAUCE 176

MUSHROOM

> CHICKEN IN WHITE WINE AND MUSHROOM
  SAUCE 160

OLIVE

> POLLOCK WITH BLACK OLIVE SAUCE 178

ONION

> TUNA ONION AND TOMATO SALAD WITH
  BORLOTTI BEANS 72
> SAUSAGE AND MASH WITH RED ONIONS
  AND HARISSA PASTE 128

PANCAKES

> PROTEIN PANCAKES 38

PASTA

> TUNA GARLIC PASTA 62
> LASAGNE 112

PEAR

> POACHED PEAR 192

PISTACHIO

> PISTACHIO CAKE 186

PIZZA

> WHOLEMEAL PIZZA BASE / NEPTUNO PIZZA /
  VEGETARIAN EGG AND ASPARAGUS PIZZA 104

POLLOCK

> POLLOCK WITH BLACK OLIVE SAUCE 178

POMEGRANATE

> POMEGRANATE PORK WITH SLOW-ROASTED
  SPICED RED CABBAGE 162

PORRIDGE

> POWER PORRIDGE WITH BLUEBERRIES AND
  PROTEIN POWDER 20

POTATO

> HEALTHY BAKED JACKET POTATO AND
  SALMON MAYONNAISE 56
> BEEF FILLET ASPARAGUS SALSA VERDE AND
  PORTUGUESE POTATOES 106
> SAUSAGE AND MASH WITH RED ONIONS
  AND HARISSA PASTE 128
> HEALTHY SHEPHERD'S PIE 130
> HEALTHY FISH AND CHIPS 138

NOTES*

> _____
> _____
> _____
> _____
> _____
> _____
> _____
> _____
> _____
> _____
> _____
> _____
> _____
> _____
> _____
> _____
> _____
> _____
> _____
> _____
> _____
> _____
> _____
> _____
> _____

ABOUT MATT LOVELL*

After qualifying as a Nutritional Therapist in 2001 Matt went on to spend time on Harley Street, specializing in elite sports, female hormonal health and body composition management.

The contacts he made through this work led to a spell, working as nutritionist with Millwall football club during which time they made the play-off for the Premiership and also qualified for the FA cup final.

In 2002 Matt started working with the England Rugby Team and was part of Clive Woodward's team that lifted the World Cup in 2003. He continues in the same role working with the England team that reached the final of the 2007 Rugby World Cup and also the 2011 World Cup Tournament.

Matt has also been working with UK Athletics since 2010 helping our track and field athletes prepare for the Olympics in 2012.

Matt works as a consultant to some leading nutrition companies, he has helped develop a range of Whey Protein powders for the Irish Company Kinetica and also advises Mule Bar on their energy bar formulations.

Matt currently runs his own elite performance based company. This is aimed at elite athletes, corporations and individuals that want to improve their health. He has written the popular Fat Loss Program **'Four Week Fat Loss'** and **'Regenerate'** a muscle building anabolic program and his blog **www.SportsNutritionVlog.com** is the most popular Sports Nutrition Resource in the UK.

Matt keeps one day a week free for seeing private clients for nutritional consultations from his office in London or via Skype. Visit **www.YourSportsNutrition.com** for further information about booking a consultation.

VISIT MY ONLINE SPORTS NUTRITION SHOP

Use the Code PSP for £5 off your first order
www.yoursportsnutrition.com

FOUR WEEK FAT LOSS

This is my best selling fat loss programme where clients lose on average 7-10 lbs of fat in a month.
www.fourweekfatloss.com

REGENERATE – MUSCLE BUILDING

This is my 12 week muscle building programme that I've used with professional athletes. This is how some Rugby players stack on 10Kg of muscle in the off season.
www.regeneratenutrition.com

SPORTS NUTRITION VLOG

My video blog site where I share the latest info from the world of Elite Sports Nutrition. Ask me any questions you have about Sports Nutrition
www.sportsnutritionvlog.com

TOXIC FAT ATTACK

Detox is a bigger area than you might think, it's not just about hangover cures. Detoxing your body can improve your PERFORMANCE.
www.sportsnutritionvlog.com/toxic-fat-attack/

MATCH DAY NUTRITION

How to get an unfair advantage by eating POWER foods and supplements that BOOST your PERFORMANCE and provide an unfair ADVANTAGE.
www.sportsnutritionvlog.com/match-day-nutrition.html

BLOOD SUGAR CONTROL

The BIGGEST THREAT to your health is not knowing how to CONTROL YOUR BLOOD SUGAR LEVEL.
www.controlbloodsugar.co.uk/

ENDURANCE NUTRITION STRATEGIES

Nutrition strategies that every endurance athlete needs to REALISE their potential.
www.sportsnutritionvlog.com/endurance-nutrition/

IMMUNITY AND NUTRITION

More athletes underperform because of this than any other reason, the ability to resist illness can often be the difference between SUCCESS AND FAILURE.
www.sportsnutritionvlog.com/immunesystem.html

FOR MORE HEALTHY RECIPES, VIDEOS OF MATT COOKING AND EXTRA RESOURCES REGARDING THE *PALM SIZED PLAN COOKBOOK* VISIT WWW.PALMSIZEDPLAN.COM

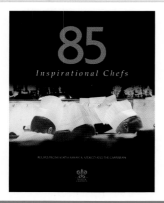
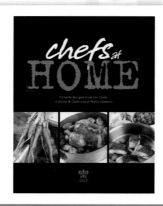
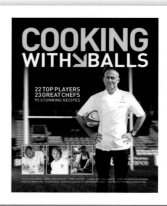
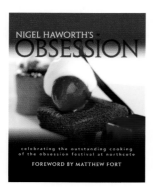

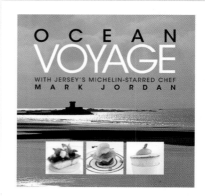